Francis Robert Raines, Thomas William King

Lancashire Funeral Certificates

Francis Robert Raines, Thomas William King

Lancashire Funeral Certificates

ISBN/EAN: 9783337417017

Printed in Europe, USA, Canada, Australia, Japan

Cover: Foto ©ninafisch / pixelio.de

More available books at www.hansebooks.com

REMAINS

HISTORICAL & LITERARY

CONNECTED WITH THE PALATINE COUNTIES OF

LANCASTER AND CHESTER.

PUBLISHED BY

THE CHETHAM SOCIETY.

VOL. LXXV.

PRINTED FOR THE CHETHAM SOCIETY.
M.DCCC.LXIX.

COUNCIL FOR 1868-9.

JAMES CROSSLEY, Esq., F.S.A., PRESIDENT.
REV. F. R. RAINES, M.A., F.S.A., HON. CANON OF MANCHESTER, VICE-PRESIDENT.
WILLIAM BEAMONT, Esq.
THE VERY REV. GEORGE HULL BOWERS, D.D., DEAN OF MANCHESTER.
R. C. CHRISTIE, Esq., M.A.
REV. THOMAS CORSER, M.A., F.S.A.
JOHN HARLAND, Esq., F.S.A.
W. A. HULTON, Esq.
WILLIAM LANGTON, Esq.
MAJOR EGERTON LEIGH.
REV. JOHN HOWARD MARSDEN, B.D., F.R.G.S., CANON OF MANCHESTER.
REV. JAMES RAINE, M.A., PREBENDARY OF YORK.
ARTHUR H. HEYWOOD, Esq., TREASURER.
R. HENRY WOOD, Esq., F.S.A., HON. SECRETARY.

LANCASHIRE FUNERAL
CERTIFICATES.

EDITED BY
THOMAS WILLIAM KING, Esq., F.S.A.,
YORK HERALD.

WITH ADDITIONS BY THE
REV. F. R. RAINES, M.A., F.S.A.,
VICE-PRESIDENT OF THE CHETHAM
SOCIETY.

PRINTED FOR THE CHETHAM SOCIETY.

M.DCCC.LXIX.

INTRODUCTION.

THE abstract of the Earl Marshal's order regarding Funeral Certificates, here printed, precludes the necessity of further observation on the subject; but perhaps it may be remarked that it is questionable whether the certificates were taken on the mere request of the executors or survivors of the deceased, or whether the Kings of arms of each province, respectively, were authorised, *nolens volens*, to enforce the order of the Earl Marshal in every or any case in which the deceased was of gentilitial rank. The probability seems to be that the practice followed the wish of the family survivors rather than that the officers of arms compelled them to conform to the Earl Marshal's orders. This opinion is strengthened from the comparatively few certificates on record throughout the kingdom. Very few indeed are preserved even of peers, these being exclusively under Garter's jurisdiction, and apparently seldom recorded in the college of arms. There is no doubt, however, that the Kings of arms had, and did exercise, jurisdiction over the armorial ensigns used at funerals, whether the formal attendance at funeral solemnities was observed, or certificates of the state of the family of the defunct were taken, as many instances occur of the exercise of such jurisdiction, and are noticed in the college books.

K.

It may be thought that some of the foot-notes, extending over several pages, are longer than the subject-matter required; but this amplification arises from a desire not to leave any thing unwritten which should really appear, nor to omit facts and miscellaneous information which would not be accessible to the general reader. If it should be thought that there is a tendency to prolixity, omission might have been culpable. Some important facts and the principal ascertained incidents of the life of each individual, have, for the first time, been brought together. Woe to him who tries to say all that can be said on any individual, even of some illustrious line, like that of Stanley, "so ancient" to adopt a remark of Gibbon in his Autobiography, "that it has no beginning, and so worthy that it ought to have no end." The annotations are restricted to the subject; and private opinions on the conduct and proceedings of the deceased have not, it is hoped, been unnecessarily or offensively obtruded on the reader. Some of the notes contain original information which may furnish future biographers with materials from which an accurate judgment may be formed of the characters, principles, and ordinary habits of life, of a few of our more distinguished Lancashire worthies, and it is trusted that this statement will be received as an exposition of the motives of the contributors of these notes.

R.

March, 1869.

CONTENTS.

Extract from the "Orders to be observide and kept by the Officers of Armes" .... *page*	1
Sir John Ratclyff, 1568	3
Edward Earl of Derby, 1572	4
Henry Earl of Derby, 1593	15
William Fleetwood, 1593	28
Henry Stanley, 1598	29
Mrs. Margaret Radcliff, 1599	35
Katherine Bretargh, 1601	37
Sir Edward Stanley, 1604	40
Edward Norres, 1606	41
Sir Alexander Barlowe, 1620	45
Sir Edmund Trafford, 1620	47
Sir Thomas Ireland, 1625	49
Robert Earl of Sussex, 1629	53
Oswald Mosley, Esq., 1630	54
Edward Moore, Esq., 1633	56
Richard Bold, Esq., 1635	58
Richard Viscount Molyneux, 1636	60
Alice Countess of Derby, 1636-7	62
George Clarke, 1637	73
Lady Dorothy Legh, 1639	80
Sir Gilbert Ireland, 1675	82
Dame Margaret Ireland, 1675	82
Sir Thomas Gerrard, 1601	88

Obscure! why prithee what am I? I knew
My father, grandsire, and great grandsire, too;
If further I derive my pedigree
I can but guess beyond the fourth degree,
The rest of my forgotten ancestors
Were sons of earth.
                    Dryden.

LANCASHIRE
FUNERAL CERTIFICATES.

EXTRACT from the " Orders to be obseruide and kepte by the " Officers of Armes made by the highe and mighty Prince " Thomas Duke of Norfolke Erle Marischall of Englande An'o " 1568 the xviiith *day of July yn the Tenth yere of the Reigne " of Queene Elizabeth."*

ITEM it is also orderid and decreed by the sayd Erle Marschall that St Gilbert Dethicke Knighte otherwise cauled Garter Principall Kinge of Armes shall haue the orderinge marshalinge and settinge forthe of the buriales of all suche noble and honorable personages as now are or at any tyme herafter shal be of the honourable order of the Garter and ther wifes in suche sorte as his Predicessors in the Offyce of Garter haue hertofor hadde and enioyed And that he shall further haue the buriales of all the nobles being peeres of this Realme and of the highe courte of Parliamente and ther wifes withe the two Archebishopes of Canterbury and Yorke and the bishope of Winchester only as also the orderinge and settinge forthe of the buriales of the heirs apparente of all Dukes, Marquesses Erles and ther Wifes. And it is forther orderide that he the sayd Garter shall take to serue with him at the funerales of the aforsayde noble and honorable personages first Clarentieulx and then Norry Kinges of Armes and so successivly one after an other the herauldes and pursuivauntes of

The Buriales appropriat and incident to Garter.

2   LANCASHIRE FUNERAL CERTICATES.

Armes in order accordinge to ther auncienty and degree in Offyce, and so to beginn agayne.

The Buriales appropriat and incedent to Clarenticulx and Norry

It is also orderede and decreede by the sayde Erle Merschall that Clarenticulx and Norry shall within ther seuerall provinces haue th' only orderinge merschalinge and settinge forthe of the funerales of all other gentill and noble personages viz. that is to say all estates from a Baron downwards excepte knightes of Th' order and ther wifes without the lette or enterruption of any other Officers of Arms and the sayd Clarienticulx and Norry shall take to serue withe them at the sayde funerales as occasion shall serue and the place requyre, other the herauldes and pursuivauntes of armes successively one after another in order accordinge to ther auncienty and degree in office. It is also orderid that Norry Kinge of Armes shall have a torne at the funerales in the province of Clarenticulx amonge the sayd heraulds and pursuivantes as the eldest heraulde. It is morouer orderid and decreed that if it shall fortune any of the Kinges of Armes to be in the Princes Service in Visitacion or sicknes or otherwise abseute that then one of the sayd Kinges of Armes to be the others Deputy as though he himself were ther presente And further it is orderide and decreed that if it fortune any of the sayd herauldes or pursuivantes to be visited withe sickness that then it shal be lawfull for every of them in tyme of sicknes to assigne his Deputy to serve for him at any suche fewnerales whiche Deputy shal be accomptable to him of all droictes and commoditycs received or hade for any such funerales. Provided also that the sayde Deputye so servinge shal be alowde his reasonable charges of him then beinge sicke any thinge in thes articles to the contrary notwithstandinge Provided alwayes that at what tyme as any of the sayd Heraulds or Pursuivauntes shall serve at any of the feonerales aforsayd the Kinge of armes not beinge present therat the sayd Herauldes or pursuivantes so servinge shall within one monithe next after the feonerall pay to the Kynge of Armes to whom it shall appertayne suche ordinary fees as at this present are vside and hertofor haue Bene accustomede.

A Deputie alowed at Funerales in cause of Sickness.

LANCASHIRE FUNERAL CERTIFICATES.   3

Item it is also orderede and decreed by the sayd Erle Marshall that every Kinge of Armes heraulde or pursuivante that shall serve at any funerall as is aforsayd shall bringe into the libiari or office of Armes a trewe and certayne Certificate vnder the hands of the executors and morners that shall be present at the sayd funerall conteyninge the day of the deathe the place of buriall of the persone so deceased. And also to whom he or she married what issewe they hade what years they were of at the tyme of the sayd buriall and to whom they were maried to th' entent that the sayd Certificate may be regestiede and so remayne as a perpetuall recorde in the sayd Office for ever. _{A Certificate to be taken at Funerales.}

Vc 1-75 SIR JOHN RATCLYFF, 1568.

Funeral Certificates, I. 5, fo. 164, Coll. Arm.

SR John Ratclyff knight 3 son to Robt Erl of Sussex deseased at his howsse at the Tower hyll in London the ixth of November in A^o 1568 and in the xth yere of the Raigne of our Soŭaigne Lady quene Elizabeth and was buryed at the pishe cherche of Saint Olyves in hart strete in the said Cytic the sixth of the said mounth and in the xth yere of the Raigne of our Soŭaigne Lady quene Elizabeth.

The said Sr John Ratclyff knight maryed Anne doughter of Thom̃ Benolt ats Clarencyeulx king of Armes and had no issue. The sole Executor to the said Sr John Ratclyff knight is the said Lady Anne his wyeff. The morners at the said fewnerall were thesse Sr Henry Ratclyff knight Mr Egremont Ratclyff his brother, Sr Henry Compton knight, Sr Henry Darcey knight and Sr Thom̃ Myldmay knight. The heraulds that served at the said ffewnerall were thesse Robert Cooke Esquyre ats Clarencyeulx kyng of Armes

Willm ffiower ats Nory kyng of Armes. Hugh Cotgrave ats Ryche-
mond heraud of Armes. In wytness that this Certyfycat is trew
I the said Lady Anne have herevnto set my hand the day and yere
above wrytten.

Vol-75   ANNE RATCLYFF.

[Sir John Radcliffe was the third son of Robert baron Fitzwalter, by
his third wife, Mary, daughter of sir John Arundell of Llanhern, in the
county of Cornwall, knight. (She afterwards married Henry Fitzalan,
the last earl of Arundel of that name.) The father of sir John (whose
funeral certificate is here given) succeeded his cousin, John Radcliffe,
esq., in 1518, in the ancient inheritance of Radcliffe tower, in Lancashire, by virtue of entail. He was created earl of Sussex on the 18th
December 1529, and was viscount and baron Fitzwalter, baron Lacy of
Egremont, Burnell and Bottetourt, lord high chamberlain of England
for life, K.G., &c. He died on the 22nd October 1542, and his third wife
on the 20th October 1557, leaving her only son, John Radcliffe, aged
18 years old at the time of his mother's death. Sir John was afterwards of Clive in the county of Somerset, and died without issue A.D.
1568, his widow, dame Anne (younger daughter and coheir of Thomas
Benholt, esq., a distinguished ambassador), surviving him, and marry-
ing, secondly, Richard Buckland, esq., by whom she had several children. She died on the 10th December 1585, and was buried at St.
Olave's, Hart-street, London. In the elaborate pedigree of the family
deduced by William Radcliffe, esq., rouge croix, Mr. Egremont Radcliffe
is described not as "the brother" but as the nephew of sir John.
(Noble's *Hist. Coll. Arms*, London, p. 111; *Hist. of Whalley*, p. 414;
Radcliffe Ped. Lanc. MSS.) R.]

EDWARD EARL OF DERBY, 1572.

Funeral Certif.   Knowsley Evid.

THE Right Honble Edward Erle of Derbye, Viscompt Kynton,
Lord Stanley, Lord Strange of Knockyn, Lord Mohun, Lord
Bassett, Lord Burnell, Lord Lacy, Lord and Kyng of Man and the

lles, one of yᵉ Lords of Her Maiesties most honᵇˡᵉ pryvie counsell and knyght companyon of yᵉ Garter, dyed att at his howse in Lancastreshyre, callyd Lathom house, on the xxiiijᵗʰ daye of October, and was buryed at Ormeskirke on the ivᵗʰ daye of Desember 1572, with greate pompe and state.

He marryed firste Dorothie, dowter to Thomas Howard Duke of Northfolk, and by her had yssue his sone and successour, the Ryght Honᵇˡᵉ Henric nowe Erle of Derbye, Syr Thomas Stanley his second sone, and Syr Edward Stanley his third sone, and also four dowters, 1 Anne, 2 Elisabeth, 3 Marie, and 4 Jane. He marryed to his second wyfe Margret, dowter of Ellis Barlowe of Barlowe, in the sayd Countie, Esquier, by whom he had issew two dowters viz. 1 Margarett and 2 Kathrein. He marryed to his third wyfe Marie, dowter to Sʳ George Cotton of Combermere, in yᵉ County of Chester, knyght, who survives him, but hath no issewe.

[On the death of his father on the 23rd May 1521, Edward lord Strange was a minor, being only in his eleventh year. He became a ward of cardinal Wolsey, who secured by grant from Henry VIII. some of the minor's estates. In 1527 the youthful earl accompanied the cardinal on his embassy to Calais. (*Wolsey Corresp.*, State Pap. vol. i. No. cviii.; *Chron. of Calais* p. 38). In 1531 he was amongst the peers who addressed the pope in favour of the king's marriage and intimated that should his holiness refuse, a remedy would be sought elsewhere. In 1532, October 11, he accompanied Henry VIII. and a large and magnificent retinue of nobles, bishops, and gentry, with their attendants, to Boulogne, where they met the French king, Francis I., the king of Navarre, the cardinal of Loraine, and the nobility of France; and amongst the gay company was the lady Anne Boleyn, marchioness of Pembroke, married to Henry VIII. in the following January. (*Chron. of Calais*, p. 43.) In 1533 he conveyed queen Anne Boleyn in his own barge from Greenwich in order to her coronation, at which solemnity he was the cup-bearer. At this time he was created a knight of the bath. September 10th 1533, at the christening of the lady Elizabeth, afterwards queen, the earl of Wiltshire and the earl of Derby supported the royal infant's train and attended the procession to the church, where archbishop Cranmer the godfather, the duchess dowager of Norfolk and the dowager marchioness of Dorset, the godmothers, and a long retinue of the nobility were present. (Nichols's *Prog.*, vol. i. p. 1.) In 1536 he took an active part in raising forces in Lancashire and Cheshire for the suppression of the pilgrimage of grace. (Nichols's *Narrative of the Reformation*, Camd. Soc., p. 284.) The king's letters addressed to him, and other unpublished documents, connected with this important northern insurrection are amongst the *Lanc. MSS.*, and will probably be printed by the CHETHAM SOCIETY. In 1539 the earl was one of the lords of the king's own train at the reception of the lady Anne of Cleves, in England, prior to her marriage with Henry VIII. (*Chron. of Calais*, p. 175.) In 1542 he marched into Scotland with Thomas Howard third duke of Norfolk, his brother-in-law, with 20,000 men, and committed great devastation. In 1544 he was a zealous supporter of the Reformation, being one of the lords appointed to further it, and also about the same time a benefactor to the church of Eccleston, in the county of Lancaster. (*Lanc. Chantries*, vol. ii. p. 179.) He was a commissioner for the dissolution of the monasteries, and amongst other spoil secured for himself, from the king, the manor and advowson of Ormskirk, which had belonged to the abbey of Burscough; but after all, the property merely returned to the family of the original donor. (Gastrell's *Not. Cestr.*, vol. ii. pt. i. pp. 196, 197.) He was also a benefactor to the church of Samlesbury in Blackburn parish (*ibid.* p. 293), but not to the Collegiate church of Manchester. (Dr. Hibbert Ware's *Hist.*, vol. i. p. 69.)

In 1546, when the high admiral of France, accompanied by a great suite, came on an embassy to the king, the earl of Derby was specially commanded by his majesty to receive the distinguished guests at Blackwall and conduct them to the court at Greenwich.

In January 1547 he was one of the mourners appointed to attend the funeral of Henry VIII. (Strype's *Mem.* vol. v. p. 269.) On the 17th February 1546-7 he was elected knight of the garter, and installed on the 22nd May following. (Beltz's *Mem. of the Order of the Garter*, p. clxxvi.)

In 1550 he was one of the peers who signed the articles of peace made between Edward VI. and the Scots and French. (Collins's [Brydges']

Peer., vol. iii. p. 71.) November 17, 1550, his mother was buried at Colham. She survived his father nearly thirty years, having married for her second husband John Radcliffe, lord Fitzwalter. She was Ann, daughter of Edward lord Hastings and Hungerford, and sister of George first earl of Huntingdon, of that name. Her first husband died at his house at Colham, in the parish of Hillingden, in the county of Middlesex, and was buried in the neighbouring monastery of Syon. She appears to have retained the popular and higher title of countess of Derby. (Machyn's *Diary*, p. 2.)

May 31, 1551, the earl of Derby arrived at Chelsea out of the north with a goodly company of men and horses. (*Ibid.* p. 6.) On the 6th July his lordship attended the king at Blackheath, accompanied by the earl of Warwick, the lord admiral Clinton, sir William Harbord, and many lords, knights, and gentlemen, and his majesty "ran at the ring," on Blackheath, and afterwards supped with the lords on board the admiral's ship at Deptford. (*Ibid.* pp. 6, 7.)

On the 8th August 1553 the "good earl of Derby" came to London to the funeral of king Edward VI. whom he had served, attended by four score men in coats of velvet, and after him two hundred and eighteen yeomen in his livery, and so to his house at Westminster. (*Ibid.* 40.)

On the 5th September 1553, the earl was appointed by queen Mary, whose cause he warmly espoused against lady Jane Grey, a judge delegate for sentence of bishop Bonner's restitution to his see. (Strype's *Mem.*, vol. iv. p. 57.) Sunday October 1, 1553, the earl was appointed high constable of England, in Westminster hall, at the coronation of queen Mary. (*Ibid.*)

On the 19th July 1554, he was one of the noblemen who, constituting a large and brilliant assemblage, attended on Philip II., prince of Spain, on his arrival in England, in order to his marriage with the queen. A full description of the pageant is given in the *Chronicle of Queen Jane and Queen Mary*, by J. G. Nichols, esq., App. p. 136, (*Camd. Soc.*) The earl was one of the three noblemen who gave her highness in marriage in the name of the whole realm. (*Ibid.* p. 169.)

In March 1555 George Marsh, the martyr, was brought before the earl of Derby and his ecclesiastical council at Lathom, where he found sir William Norris of Speke, sir Piers Legh of Lyme, master Sherburn

the rector of Grappenhale, master More, and others; and the earl
closely examined him on controverted points of theology. He was sent
to "a cold and windy stone room," and left in solitary confinement at
Lathom, until Palm Sunday, when the earl, sir John Byron, and the
vicar of Prescot again sent for and sharply catechised him. The earl
afterwards said to Marsh that he, lord Windsor, and lord Dacre, who
had been reputed advocates of the Reformation, had never consented
to the acts of religion in the time of Edward VI. There visited him in
his cell at Lathom Mr. Westby, Mr. Ashaw of the Hill, Mr. Assheton
of Chadderton, and other influential and earnest minded men of the
reformed faith. (Foxe's *Martyrs*, vol. vii. pt. 1. p. 42 *et seq.*)

In 1555 John Bradford the learned and devout Manchester martyr,
was visited in prison by Dr. Weston the Roman catholic dean of Westminster, at the request of the earl of Derby. He was accompanied by
one of the earl's men and by Dr. Collyer, once warden of Manchester;
afterwards Dr. Pendleton the Grammar schoolmaster, Stephen Beck a
wealthy merchant, and the said Dr. Collyer, all Manchester men, well
acquainted with the popular feeling on the subject, and opposed to his
creed, visited Bradford. (*Ibid.* pp. 182-184, *Ch. Histor.*) Pendleton and
Beck were relatives of Bradford, and of Roger Beswick his brother-in-
law. (See *Hist. of Lanc. Chantries*, vol. ii. p. 248, note; Wood's *Athen.*
[Bliss] vol. i. p. 325.) For an account of the earl's treatment of two
heads of the Roman catholic party in Lancashire see *Stanley Papers*,
pt. iii. p. cxxvii., note 52.

In 1557 the earl of Derby received letters from the earl of Shrewsbury authorising him to muster and prepare the inhabitants of the
counties of Lancaster and Chester to be ready to repair to the earl
with his servants and tenants and such force as he should be able to
make to serve their majesties, in such order and place as the earl of
Shrewsbury for the time should appoint. (Strype's *Mem.* vol. v. p. 227.)
On the 20th September 1557 he wrote again to the earl of Derby lord
lieutenant of the counties of Lancaster and Chester, to let him know
that according to such information as he had received the Scots intended
to have an army consisting of the whole force of Scotland in readiness
within two days of Michaelmas day, and therewith to invade England
if not resisted. Therefore he required lord Derby with all speed to come
forward with the whole force of Lancashire and Cheshire, and to be with

the said force at Newcastle, on the 5th October. The earl of Derby on the 22nd September, sent word to the lord lieutenant, that he intended to set forward upon Thursday the last of September, and to proceed with the best speed he could, lying the first night at Blackburn, the second at Gisburne, and the third at Skipton, or near those places, trusting his lordship would have consideration to give order for payment of coat and conduct money as he had been accustomed in time past, remembering the simple and poor estate of the subject at that time who otherwise were likely to be in great want. (*Ibid.* p. 229.) The earl of Derby conducted the Lancashire and Cheshire men in such great numbers that the queen, dreading the excessive charges, forbade the earl to go forwards, and commanded him to keep his forces at home, determining for the present to resist the Scots' doings with a less force than the whole army, and this, notwithstanding the lord president's former letter to him addressed, but yet to remain in perfect readiness to come forward hereafter, if occasion required, upon any sudden warning. This good husbandry in this imminent danger, and countermanding his orders, did not much please the said lord president nor the earl of Derby. (*Ibid.*) Strype gives the names of the Lancashire and Cheshire captains and the number of their men, which was about 3,200.

November 17th, 1558 queen Mary died, and her successor, Elizabeth, prudently retained thirteen of the late queen's privy councillors, amongst whom was the earl of Derby; and on the 21st the marquis of Winchester and the earls of Shrewsbury and Derby were specially summoned, by mandate from the queen sitting in council at Hatfield house, to attend her majesty on her first entrance into London with all their train and servants, and with such of the nobility whose names were inclosed, being at that time in London. (Nichols's *Prog. Q. Eliz.* vol. i. p. 35.)

The earl lost his second wife, Margaret, daughter of Ellis Barlow of Barlow, near Manchester, esq., M.P., on the 19th January, and she was buried on the 24th February 1558-9, at Ormskirk, with great solemnity, attended by knights, squires, and gentlemen, ladies and gentlewomen, yeomen in black coats and coat armour, in gold and silver, with standards, banners, and flags, "right pleasant to beholde," the lady Margaret (her elder daughter), being the chief mourner. Dr. Thomas Stanley, bishop of Man being present, sang a solemn mass on that day, having on his ornaments and mitre. On the Tuesday following, 40*l.* was dealt out " for her sowle," to the poor of eight parishes. Richard Sheale, a local minstrel, sang her praises in an "Epitaph," of which a short specimen may be given:

> O Lathom, Lathom, thowe must lament, for thowe hast lost a floware,
> For Margaret, the Countes of Darbe in the yerth hast bylte her boware.
>   *   *   *   *
> Farewell my louinge brothar Barlowe, my leve I tak of thee.
> Wyth these mortale yeys that I now bear, noe more I shall you see.
> Fetch me the goode Stanley, sayd she   .   .   .
> Good Sir Thomas Stanley, she sayd, yᵗ is so lyke my lorde.
> A messenger then for was made to foche yᵗ gentyll knyght,
> But or he to Latham came yᵗ was abowt midnyght,
> When that he saw yᵗ she was dede he wept and made gret sorrow,
> For he lovyde her well and she lovyde him, all this is ryght well knowen.
>   *   *   *   *
> To *Ormykyrke* was her bodye brought and there was wrapt in clay.
>   *   *   *   *

It appears that the countess, aware of her approaching death, gave wise maternal counsel to her daughter, the lady Margaret, and enjoyned her to be good towards her younger sister Katherine, these being her two daughters by the earl, exhorted her children to serve God day and night, and always to be charitable to the poor. She also took an affectionate farewell of her two step-daughters, the lady Mary and lady Jane. These four children of the earl appear to have been present at the closing scene. The earl is not named. (*Palatine Garland*, p. 49.)

The earl soon married again. His third wife was Mary, daughter of sir George Cotton of Combermere, knight, vice-chamberlain of the household of prince Edward, and K.G., by whom he had no issue. On the 1st January 1561–2 queen Elizabeth presented a new year's gift to the earl of Derby, being " one guilt bowl with a cover, per oz. 31 oz. ¼ dim. and to the countess of Derby one guilt cup with a cover, per oz. 23½, dim. ¼ oz.," whilst the earl gave at the same time to her majesty in " a purse of crimson satten, embraudered with gold in dimy. 20*l.*," and the countess offered, in " a purse of crimson satten, embrodered with gold in dimy. 10*l.*" (Nichols's *Prog. of Eliz.* vol. i.)

April 22nd, 1563, being St. George's day, the knights of the garter came from the queen's chamber, through the hall, to her chapel, which was strewn with green rushes, and amongst others came the earl of Derby, and every knight went to his own stall. Afterwards there was a great procession preceded by all the heralds and sergeants of arms, the duke of Norfolk, master garter, and master Norres the dean of the chapel, being arrayed in crimson satin velvet; then came the bishop of Winchester and sir William Petre in robes of crimson velvet with red crosses on their robes. The earl of Northumberland bare the sword, and then came the queen in her robe, and master Knollys bare the queen's train. (Machyn's *Diary*, p. 305.)

His *Household Expenses* in Lancashire for the year 1561 and his *Household Regulations* for the year 1568 have been printed by the CHETHAM SOCIETY. There is in the volume a finely etched portrait of the earl, from the original picture at Worden hall. He is said by Hollinshed to have died November 24th, 1573, an. reg. 14 Eliz., (vol. ii. p. 1257,) which is an error corrected by this funeral certificate. He offered to raise 10,000 at his own charge for the suppression of the rebellion of the two northern earls. He never forced any service at his tenants' hands but always due payment of their rent. His liberality to strangers and to such as showed themselves grateful to him was remarkable. No gentleman ever waited in his service without allowance, as well wages as otherwise, for horse and man. His annual household expenses amounted to 4,000*l*., and Camden says, (*Hist. of Queen Eliz.*, p. 188,) "with him the glory of hospitality hath in a manner fallen asleep." He was famous for his cunning in setting bones, disjointed or broken, and also for his skill in surgery, and a desire to help the poor. Conscious of his approaching dissolution he took a final leave of all his servants before his death by shaking of hands and reminding them of the last day. (*Hollinshed*, vol. ii. p. 1258.)

The magnificent ceremonial of this nobleman's funeral was probably greater than that of any contemporary peer, and more than rivalled the royal exequies. The details have often been printed in the *Peerages* from a manuscript of John Anstis, esq., garter. He is erroneously said, first by Collins and by all subsequent writers, to have died in the year 1574. Hollinshed and Stow also erroneously state that he fed 2700 persons with meat and drink every "Good Friday" during thirty-five years. The great festival of Christmas was clearly intended, and not the fast-day of the crucifixion of our Saviour. The following abstract of his will, which has not before been printed, contains several curious particulars relating to his immediate family connections and domestic arrangements.

It is dated the 28th of August 1572 (not the 24th as in sir Egerton Brydges' edition of Collins's *Peerage*), and was proved in Doctors' Commons by all the executors therein named on the 21st November. He is styled in the probate "of Lathom in the County of Lancaster and Diocese of Chester, deceased," and from the copy of the funeral certificate it appears that he died there. He states himself to be at the time of making his will "of good and p̃fecte mynde p̃ remẽbrance," but knowing "that it is mete p̃ convenyant for everye creature so to prepaire that they be alwayes redye as though death showlde sodenlye come," he makes his will. "First I surender p̃ beqweath my sowle vnto Almyghtye God the Savio⁹ p̃ Redymer of mankinde, and my bodye to be buryed in the earth w^{th}in the P'ish Churtche of Ormeschurtche, in the plase where hit maye be thought convenyent at the discresyon of my Executors." And for the payment of his debts and the preferment of his children, kinsfolks and servants not then preferred or holpen, and for the discharge of his funerals, "and the errecting p̃ bvlding of one Chappell p̃ one Monvmente or Towmbe at Ormeschurtche for the bvryall of my corpes according to my honowre and vocation," he gives and bequeaths to his executors in trust, "his Manors of Wetton, Thraylles, Awlston, Anlesargh, Raineforth, Clawghton, Thorncley, Osmownderley, Torrisholme, Oxcliffe, Cople, Chorley, Bolton en le Mores, Vlueswalton p̃ Kellermore, in the County of Lancaster; his Manors of Bythome and Arnesheade, in the County of Westmereland; his Manor of Borton in Lonsdale, in the County of York; his Manor of Malowrsarseneck, in the County of Flint; his Manors of Midle alias Mowld, Nostrandge and Nesklyffe, in the County of Salop," with sundry messages, lands, rents, &c., for the performance of his will. "And my Wille is that my saide Executowrs shall w^{th}in convenyent tyme after my dissease cawse one cõvenyent Chappell to be bvlded p̃ made at the P'rish Churtche of Ormeschurtche, and a Towmbe there for my corpes or body to be layde in mete for my honowre p̃ calling." He gives out of the said manors an annuity of ten pounds to Mawd Scaresbryke for her life; to his servant Hugh Holme a similar annuity of 4*l.*; to George Moscroppe an annuity of 4*l.*; to his four servants Dormyssyvs Vlster an annuity of 3*l.* 6*s.* 8*d.*; to Robert Talbot an annuity of 4*l.*; to Rawffe Hollande four marks; to Nicholas ffyñcy 3*l.* 6*s.* 8*d.* Also to his lordship's "Cossin Katherine Storton for herr mayntenanse, advansement ę preferment in maryadge, the some of fowre hvndreth markes, to be levied ę taken of the issves ę p'fitts of my sayde Manowrs, lands, tenym^{ts} ę heredittamentes." He bequeaths to his servant Henry Morecrofte 10*l.* After the payments of debts and legacies the remainder of his manors, &c., is devised to his son Henry lord Strandge, and the heirs male of his body, lawfully begotten, and in default of such issue, to the right heirs of the said earl of Derby for ever. And he appoints his "Ryght welbeloved S'vantes S' Petter Leigh, S' Ryc. Shyrborne, Knyghtes, Wm Massey, Henry Stanley, Alexander Barlowe, Esquires, Alexander Rigbye and Wm Stopforth, Gentlemen, Executors;" and constituted "the Right Honorable his verye good Lordes the Earle of Sussex ę the Earle of Leyster" Supervisors. He bequeaths to Anne Hawarden 20*l.* to be paid unto her in money, and to his servant Marmaduke Newton 6*l.* 13*s.* 4*d.* yearly, "during the continuance of W^m ffarington his Lease of my moyety or halfe p'te of Vlneswalton." "Also to my son Thomas my best Horse, to my son Edward my best Gelding, to my daughter Morley 10*l.* in plate, to my daughter Stafforth the money that my son Stafforth her husband oweth me by his Bill, to my daughter Stafforth 10*l.* in plate, to my daughter Margaret 40*l.* in money or plate, to my son the Lord Storton 100 marks, to my son[1] fferdinando 20*l.*, to my son[1] Wm Stanley 10*l.*, to my son[1] Francis Stanley 10*l.*, to my son Edward Parker 10*l.* in plate, to my cousin Henry Stanley 40*l.* which he owes me by Bill, to each of my Executors 6*l.* 13*s.* 4*d.*, and to each of my Supervisors a piece of plate of 20*l.* Also it is my Will that my Executors shall disburse among poor People as by their discretions shall be thought meet. Also to my servants of Houschold attending in my house that be not preferred by me with lease, annuity or otherwise, to have every of them a year's wages. I will and devise that my daughter Margaret shall have and enjoy my farm and demesne lands of Childwall during her life. I give to my daughter Strandge a silver cup of the value of 10*l.*, to my son[1] Edward Stanley son of my said son Tho-

---

[1] It is remarkable that he styles all his grandsons his sons.

mas 6*l*. 13*s*. 4*d*. in money or plate, to my son John Dvdley his nurse 6*l*. 13*s*. 4*d*. in money, to my servant Rawfe Birkenhead 6*l*. 13*s*. 4*d*. a y^r for life, to my servant Ewan Carre 6*l*. 13*s*. 4*d*. a year, to Wm Humfraye my son Strandge his servant 6*l*. 13*s*. 4*d*. a year, to Claras Stopforth 6*l*. 13*s*. 4*d*. a year for life, to the right Honorable ᵽ my very good Lord Bvrleye, Lord High Treasurer of England, one piece of plate to the value of 20*l*. in token of remembrance. These persons were present at the publishing and ensealing of this present Will — John Storton, Thomas Vavisour, Doctor, John Sherbourn, John Eggerton, Wm Stanley, Wm Orrell, Tho. Gillibrownde." There are some brief notices of the earl in the MS. " Geneal. Collections," of Edward thirteenth earl of Derby, K.G., at Knowsley.

In reviewing the character and proceedings of this great earl we may fairly infer that he was an able statesman and a wily politician, unsettled in his religion and Erastian in his views, an economist of time, discrete, humane, and every where popular, especially in Lancashire.

AN EPITAPHE UPON THE DEATHE OF THE RIGHT HONORABLE EDWARD STANLEY, EARLE OF DERBIE, &c.

Harl. MS. 2129, *fol.* 35.

²Behold heare lieth close in clay	He also Earle of Derbie was
a wight of worthy fame	As his forfathers weare
Of statelie stock of Lordlie lyne	Wher he no lesse authoritie
³and Stanleigh was his name	then they before did beare
In Man he ruled as King and ther	Then Knight of Garter he was made
did use sutch holsome Lawe	⁵a noble ord^r sure
As those that ⁴guyded und^r him	Lo his deserts at Princes handes
wth ease kept them in awe	sutch favor did procure.

² On the right hand side of this MS. epitaph there is a repetition, with the following trifling variations :

        Behould in mould full could now lyeth
        a wight of worthy fame
   ³ that Stanley had to name
        In Man as prince he ruld and ther
        did hold such holsome law
   ⁴ govern'd   ⁵ the

And lyving in prosperitie
devoid of care and striffe
And fortune fawning thus on him
in man{.sup r} all his liffe
Could Pompous pride or glorie vaine
from vertue drawe his mynde
No, he never did degenerat
from that he was by kynd
Or did he cease to ayde the poore
wth meate wth tong wth hand
No sure his like in all respectes
was not w'in this laud
How many lame and impotent
did he wth paine and toile
Reduce unto their former health
wthin his countrey soile
How manye did hee dailie feede
whom neede had prickt before
How many have yo^w now alyve
so carefull for the poore?
How liberall was hee unto his men
how carefull for his frend
How good unto his tenants still
even to his latter ende

Oh God his faith unto his Prince
surmounting was allwayes
As well was knowen by that hee did
in those his latter daies
All vertuous actes he did declare
and vyces dyd detest
What should I say, Amongst the good
he was accompted best.
He causeth now the poore to mourne
w^t many a weeping eye
His men his frendes his tenannts eke
to mourne themselves applie
Our noble Queene bewailes the losse
of such a precious perle
A thousand tymes no doubt she says
hee was a noble earle!
In health and sicknes well he lyvde
and well he tooke his ende
Would God eich one would learne by him
their spotted lyffes to mend
The heaven doth now possesse his soule
the earthe his corps retayns
His passed lyfe a looking glasse
for others yet Remayns.

FINIS.

R.]

HENRY EARL OF DERBY, 1593.

Funeral Certif. Knowsley Evid.

THE Ryght Honble Henrye Erle of Derbye Lord Stanley and Strange of Knockin, Lord and Governour of the Isle of Man and the Isles, Knight of the most Noble Order of ye Garter, Chamberlain of the Citye and Countye of Chester and one of the Quenes Maiesties hon^{ble}able Privye Counsell deceased att his house called Lathome in Lancashire on ye 25th daye of September in ye yere of our Lord 1593 and was hon^{ble}ably buryed at Ormeschurch with his auncestors.

He married Margarett sole childe to Henrie Erle of Cumber-
land by his wife Alianore one of ye dowters and coheires of Charles
Duke of Suffolk, K.G., by his wife Marie, youngest dowter to
Kinge Henry VII. and sometyme Queene dowager of France.

By his saide wife, who still survives, he had issewe 1 Edward
Lord Strange, who died when younge, 2 Ferdinando, son and heyre,
now Erle of Derby, and who ys wedded and hath issewe, 3 Francis,
who predeceased his father, 4 William the youngest sone as yett
unmaryed.

The ffuncrall obseruances and ceremonyes were prosecuted about
this moost noble personage cheiflye by one who felt well his un-
worthynes and unhabylyties to engage soe grete a mater.

[Henry Stanley, lord Strange, was the son and heir of Edward third
earl of Derby, K.G., by his first wife, the lady Dorothy Howard,
daughter of Thomas, second duke of Norfolk, and was born about
the year 1533. On the 20th of February, 1548, being shrove Sunday,
he was made knight of the bath by Edward VI., that being the day of
his coronation. (Strype's *Mem.* vol. v. p. 309.) As soon as he attained
his majority he married, on the 7th February 1554-5, lady Margaret
[Clifford] only daughter of Henry 12th baron de Clifford, and 2nd
earl of Cumberland, and of his wife, the lady Eleanor, daughter and
coheiress of Charles Brandon, duke of Suffolk, K.G., by his wife Mary,
queen dowager of France and sister of king Henry VIII. Lord
Strange's marriage took place at Whitehall chapel, in the presence of
the king and queen. There was afterwards at the court a great dinner,
and jousts, and a tournament on horseback, with swords. After
supper, was introduced "juego de canas," or tilting with canes, a
Spanish amusement, patronized by king Philip, with torchlights and
cresset lights — sixty cressets and one hundred torches — and the
whole concluding with a mask and a banquet. (Machyn's *Diary*,
edited by J. G. Nichols, F.S.A., p. 82.)

On the 23rd April 1557, being St. George's day, king Philip and
queen Mary attended mass, solemnised by the bishop of Winchester,
and Lord Strange bare the sword of state at evensong. (*Ibid.* p. 135.)

On the 25th October 1561, lord Strange and others were appointed to conduct the French ambassadors on their way from Scotland, to queen Elizabeth, then at the earl of Bedford's, with a thousand horse, through Fleet street, and the ambassadors were afterwards entertained by the queen at Whitehall with the not very feminine amusement of bull and bear baiting. (*Ibid.* p. 270.)

On the 1st January 1561-2, lady Margaret Strainge gave a new year's gift to the queen of a little round mount of gold to contain a pomander in it. (*Harl. MS., quoted in* Nichols's *Prog. of Queen Eliz.* vol. i.) On the same day the queen presented new year's gifts to the earl and countess of Derby, and also to the lady Margaret Strange, "one guilt bolle with a couer per oz. 16 oz. ¾ dim."

On the 13th April 1564 peace was concluded between England and France, and shortly afterwards the queen sent her choleric kinsman Henry Carey lord Hunsdon, then the lord chamberlain, as ambassador, to invest the king with the noble order of the garter. He was accompanied to France by the young lord Strange and others, who, finding the king at Lyons on a progress, there executed their commission. (Holinshed's *Chron.*, vol. iii. p. 1206.) In August of the same year the queen visited the university of Cambridge, and was intellectually entertained by disputations, orations, sermons, and theatricals, and displayed her own scholarship by delivering an elaborate latin speech to the university. Amongst the ladies of her train was Margaret, lady Strange, who was accommodated, with other persons of distinction, in the Fellows' chambers in King's college. (Nichols's *Prog. of Queen Eliz.*, vol. i.) On the 25th December 1565 the queen attended divine service in state, and received the holy communion, the sword being borne by the earl of Warwick, and her majesty's train of purple velvet, embroidered with silver very richly set with stones, was borne by the lady Strange. (*Ibid.* p. 199.)

In 1565 Henry lord Berkeley bought a lute of mother of pearl for his lady, for which queen Elizabeth had offered one hundred marks. This lute, lord Berkeley, when a widower, about ten years afterwards gave to the countess of Derby. . . . This same lute was about the year 1810 in the possession of Mrs. Jordan the actress, who had bought it at a sale. (Fosbroke's *Extracts from the Berkeley MSS.*, p. 192.)

On the 31st August 1566 the queen visited Oxford university, and two days before her coming thither the marquis of Northampton, Dudley earl of Leicester, the chancellor of the university, lord Strange, sir William Cecil, and others, repaired to Oxford to see what provision had been made for her majesty's entertainment. Their own entertainment and reception during their stay were, however, much damped by its "raining vehemently," notwithstanding which Cecil found an opportunity of inquiring of the learned Mr. Pottes why Aristotle wrote *De Monarchia*, there being at that time no monarch in the world. On the 6th September a convocation was held, and several distinguished noblemen and gentlemen were created and incorporated masters of arts, amongst the rest Henry lord Strange.

October 24th 1572 he succeeded his father as fourth earl of Derby, being at that time in his fortieth year. On the 1st January 1572-3 the new year's gifts to queen Elizabeth by the lady Margaret countess of Derby consisted of "First, twoe juelles of golde, the one being an Oystego [? oyster egg] garnished with two blue saphers, sundry smale diamondes and rubyes with two perles hanging by a smale cheine at a knotte having two dyamones and rubyes thearat; thother boing a little tablet of golde haveing thearin a spyder and a flye of ophalle, with one perle pendaunte like two. The same delivered by her Majesties commaundement to the Lady Mary Vere." (Nichols's *Prog. of Queen Eliz.*, vol. i.)

April 24th 1574 the earl was elected one of the knights of the garter, and was installed at Windsor with Henry Herbert earl of Pembroke on the 20th May following. (Beltz's *Memor.*, p. clxxxi.) The warrant for his robes as K.G. is dated 17th May 1574. (*Add. MS.*, 5756, f. 227.) In 1576 he was summoned to parliament and took his seat on the 8th February in the same year. He and the high commissioners of the queen assembled in Manchester and issued stringent orders against pipers, minstrels, and bull baitings on Sabbath days, wakes and feasts.

January 1st 1577-8. "Geven to the Queen by therle of Darby in golde 20*l*. and presented by the Queen to the Lady Margaret Countes of Darby one dooble booles [bowl] guilte. Brandon, [probably plate which had belonged to the Brandon family] per oz. 50 oz. and Her Majesty presented to the Earl of Darby thre booles with a cover of silver and guilte, per oz. 30 oz."

January 1st, 1578-9. "Presented to the Queen by the Lady Margaret Countes of Derby, a trayne gowne of tawny velvett." (Nichols's *Prog. of Queen Eliz.*, vol. i.) Notwithstanding this exchange of new year's gifts and the apparent mutual feeling of regard, the countess of Derby in the year following was cruelly suspected of disloyalty to the queen, and, being placed in some sort of confinement, sorrowfully complained of the hardship, and styled herself "her majesty's prisoner." (*Harl. MS. cod.* 787, f. 166.)

In 1579 the earl chiefly resided, from political motives, at Alport lodge in Manchester, and was associated with bishop Chaderton, sir Richard Sherburne, sir John Radcliffe, and sir Edward Fitton, in executing the penal laws against recusants, and in 1581 those gentlemen, along with the earl, were commissioners for compounding with the tenants of the college of Manchester who had obtained fraudulent leases of the tithes and other possessions of that plundered church. (Peck's *Desid. Cur.*, lib. iv. fol.)

In May 1580 his wife, who had suffered for some time from rheumatism, or some similar affection, and had employed an unprincipled medical man who resided in her house, was scandalously charged by him with disloyalty to the queen, and she was forthwith placed under restraint, and committed to an easy surveillance, but called by her "a prison." Her own letter to Walsingham on the subject is published in sir Harris Nicholas's *Life of Hatton*. With the queen her crime was not being addicted to the fashionable art of astrology or of tenebrous necromancy, but in truth, her being the daughter of the lady Eleanor Brandon, and too near the succession.

On the 26th January 1584-5 the earl was appointed by the queen to invest Henry III. king of France, with the order of the garter, and having taken leave of her majesty at Greenwich on the 20th, he passed through London with a splendid retinue of lords and nobles. (*Stanley Papers*, pt. ii. introd. p. xlix.) Holinshed gives a journal of all the proceedings until his lordship's return to England on the 12th March following, and says that the earl made no speech to the French king, and yet in *Cotton MS. Calig.* E. vii. f. 230-1 is a copy of the speech, either made or intended to be made on Thursday the 18th February, when the investiture took place, which was at evensong, as the earl and his companions refused to be present at the mass. (Camden's *Eliz.*, book iii. p. 305.)

On the 20th June 1585 the lords of the council assembled at Greenwich, Henry earl of Derby being present, and addressed a letter to
Ferdinando lord Strange, bishop Chaderton, and the other Lancashire
and Cheshire magistrates, complaining that several libels had been
formerly published against the queen, and that lately a "most vile,
slanderous, hatefull and infamous book" had been published against
her right trusty and well beloved cousin Robert, earl of Leicester,
called *Leicester's Commonwealth*, and requiring that it should be sup-
pressed. Leicester's connection with the two northern palatinates
induced him to use his influence with the queen to obtain this injunction, as the attacks upon his character, principles, and objects,
were, Camden cautiously says, "not without mixture of some un-
truths," widely circulated. (Camden's *Annals of Eliz.*, p. 419; Forbes'
State Papers, p. 711.)

The earl was always alive to the importance of the maritime defences
of the country, and seems to have had the most precise information on
the subject. He possessed, in MS., "The Booke of the whole Navye,"
containing the names of all the queen's ships, with their tonnage,
number of mariners, gunners and soldiers, dated the 27th December
1585. The whole navy at that time consisted of thirty-six ships. He
also had another MS. list, called "A Book of the Numbers, Names and
Burden of all the Ships, Barques and Vessels, with the names of all
Masters and able Mariners belonging thereto, within or appertaining
to the River of Chester." This book was written by William Wall,
the mayor, in February 1586, by the command of the earl of Derby,
to whom it is dedicated. It appears that all the vessels amounted to
fifteen. To this is subjoined a similar account of the barques belonging
to the river near Preston, in Lancashire, called the water of the Ribble,
written by Laurence Walle, mayor of Preston, at the command of the
earl of Derby, the lord-lieutenant of the county. The number of
vessels was eight. There is also an account of the vessels belonging
to the river Wyer, in Lancashire, addressed to the earl in the same
year, by Henry Butler, esq., and William Skillicorne, gent. The number was twenty-eight. This is followed by another account of the
vessels belonging to the Peel of Fouldrey and its creeks, in Furnes
and Cartmell in the county of Lancaster, addressed to the earl, in the
same year, by John Bradley, esq., and John Richardson, gent. The

number of vessels was only five. To this succeeds a list of all the vessels in the port of Liverpool, taken in the same year, with the names of the places to which they were bound, and the owners, mariners, &c. The number was twenty-eight. All these enquiries were made by the earl at the request of the Privy council, in the prospect of the Spanish invasion, which led to the granting of an entire subsidy, as well as two fifteenths and tenths, by the parliament, the first payment of which was to be made in November 1587, and the second in November 1588. The lord-lieutenant appointed the collectors for Lancashire, and they were selected from his deputy-lieutenants and justices of the peace. (*Sloane MS.*) The original assessment with the sums paid by the inhabitants of the hundred of Salford is amongst the *Lanc. MSS.* at Milnrow vicarage.

The earl obtained at the same time "A List of all the Soldiers and Munition in the Castle of Rushen and Castle Peel in the Isle of Man," and was informed of the provisions wanting there. At the same time a hope was expressed that his lordship would speedily supply the same. And to this is added the number of all sorts of serviceable men within the said island. The number of horsemen was 41, calliver-men 18, bowmen 286, and bill-men 357, but all much unprovided with weapons and other furniture, as appeared by the signatures of R. Sherburne, H. Scarisbricke, W. Lucas, T. Burscoghe and H. Radclyffe. (*Ibid.*)

On October 14th 1586, being of the privy council, he sat in the hall of Fotheringay as president, on the trial of the queen of Scots, his wife's cousin, being one of the twenty-five peers who passed sentence on that unfortunate queen, after her wearisome and harsh captivity. The sanction of the earl to that foul deed which terminated the long inevitable fate of Mary could not fail to be peculiarly acceptable to Elizabeth. The two queens were the representatives of the two great divisions of the church, and it would hardly be expected that the strong Anglican views of earl Henry would allow his more benignant feelings and gentler sympathies to prevail over his sincere religious convictions. That he was influenced in his policy by the external pressure of the court, in what he deemed an indispensable necessity and a public duty to the state, seems indisputable, although he considered, like all dupes, that his judgment was independent. There is evidence to prove that he had paid great attention to the whole of the proceedings against the queen of Scots, as amongst his evidences are found "Arguments for the sudden execution of Mary Queen of Scots," but whether this was the production of his lordship or merely a document placed in his hands to furnish him with arguments in favour of the measure, is unknown. (*Sloane MS.* 874.) The writer opens his dissertation by asserting that it was useless to adduce reasons in favour of a measure which, he assumed, was indispensably necessary, and that it were irrational to suppose that it might safely be deferred. His lordship had also carefully transcribed queen Elizabeth's speech in parliament in 1586, concerning the "Form of proceeding against the Queen of Scots, and her Majesty's reasons for delaying the execution of Mary in reply to the Petition of the Commons." (*Ditto in Oldys.*) This was an elaborate and well written speech, and embraced such points as were likely to be acceptable to the nation, nor did the artful queen omit to inform her faithful subjects that she had withheld the fatal warrant until "she had at first with earnest prayer besought the Divine Majesty so to illuminate her understanding and inspire her with his grace that she might do that which would establish the church, preserve their estates, and conduce to the prosperity of the country." The religious tone, which was not adopted without due consideration, was a sensational appeal to prejudices and feelings already deeply excited against the queen of Scots and her religious creed.

The earl had also collected "Historical examples of precedents of Sovereign Princes being condemned and put to death in a formal and advised manner, from reasons of State," and a comparison was instituted between the cases adduced and that of the queen of Scots; nor had he omitted noticing some grave and startling instances of popes, vested, as they affirmed, with infallibility, who had solemnly given their judgment for the execution of kings, and what was still more startling, but scarcely so much to the purpose, that Urban VIII. not only put to death eight cardinals, his brethren, but having their bodies reduced to powder carried them about with him in portmanteaus, and had their purple hats borne in state before him, as a warning and example to traitors! The authorities are all duly cited, and were considered to bear upon the case of the royal prisoner at Fotheringay. The earl's near family connection with queen Mary could not fail to strengthen, in the estimation at least of the reflecting part of the public, the apparent justice of Elizabeth's proceedings, and to deepen the impression of Mary's presumed guilt.

The earl had also in his possession (*Sloane MS.* 874) a copy of the speech of queen Elizabeth in answer to the French ambassador, monsieur Delievre, and the rest of his company, justifying her proceedings against queen Mary. She averred that her sorrow on the deaths of her father, of the king her brother, and of the queen her sister, had been less than that occasioned by the death of Mary her cousin of Scotland, and although she did not employ her "great oath" to corroborate her assertion, she adopted language scarcely less strong.

Amongst the earl's papers was found a MS. entitled "The Manner of the Execution of the Queen of Scots the 8 of Feb^r 1586-7, in the presence of such whose names are underwritten," and contains the well known details of that gloomy tragedy. (*Sloane MS.* 874; *earl of Derby's Hist. Collect.*; Oldys' *Brit. Libr.*)

On the 5th July 1587 the earl was fixed upon as ambassador to the court of France, and he requested that lord Burghley would give him timely notice. He was summoned to appear at court previous to his embassy, and that interview appears to have cancelled the appointment. (*Lansd. MS.*, 53, 56.) He was afterwards appointed, in September 1587, ambassador to the Low countries, and was accompanied by certain commissioners, to treat of peace with the prince of Parma, general of the forces of the king of Spain, in Flanders; and on the 1st December 1587 he solicited lord Burghley for a loan of 1000*l.* to support his embassy. (*Lansd. MS.* 16-66.) In 1587-8 he wrote to the earl of Leicester notifying his arrival at Ostend. (*Cotton MS. Vesp.* cviii. f. 100. He does not appear to have been an active or vigorous diplomatist, but he punctually executed his orders and enjoyed the personal friendship of the sovereign of his own country, and was evidently respected by the sovereigns of France and Spain. There is no reason to doubt that he was not only an able but an upright and honourable administrator. He was not unworthy to be the friend of Cecil and to be associated with the virtuous Chaderton, and one of the best acts of his life was his personal interposition with queen Elizabeth to restore and preserve the ruined, despoiled and disendowed Collegiate church of Manchester, especially when that act is referred to the low standard of the times in which he lived. (*Stanley Pap.*, vol. ii. p. cclxxxi.

note.) He shared in the councils of the great statesmen of the day, and seems to have been, upon the whole, implicitly trusted by them in the events of a most critical and exciting period of our history.

On the 14th April 1589, Philip Howard, earl of Arundel, eldest son of Thomas, fourth duke of Norfolk, K.G., was frivolously arraigned of high treason, and at this date the earl of Derby was constituted lord high steward of England at the trial, which took place in Westminster hall before twenty-five of his peers. The subject matter was chiefly connected with the queen of Scots and cardinal Allen. The earl was feebly convicted and attainted, but not executed. He died in prison. Lord Derby was first cousin of Catherine Howard the fifth queen of Henry VIII. He was also first cousin of Henry earl of Surrey, the celebrated poet, the grandfather of the attainted earl of Arundel, and we may hope that this relationship had some influence in saving the young and harshly-treated earl of Arundel from the disastrous fate of his father and grandfather.

In 1589 the earl was appointed by queen Elizabeth, chamberlain of the city and county palatine of Chester, and continued in that ancient and honourable office until his death. (*Chetham Miscell.* vol. II. p. 30.)

The *Household Regulations* of the earl and an interesting *Diary* containing the names of his intimate friends and guests in Lancashire, from the year 1572 to 1590, have been printed by the CHETHAM SOCIETY. There is also in the same volume an excellent etching of his portrait from the original at Worden hall, an autograph letter, and some notices of his domestic proceedings. He had issue by his wife three sons, two of whom successively inherited the titles, but having lived unhappily with her in private life, her name nowhere occurs in his social and domestic circle, nor in that of his father, whilst they resided in Lancashire. Neither is it to be named to his credit that, surrounded by austere puritan preachers and active protestant laymen, he had more than one mistress. Several of his natural children were recognized, educated, preferred and settled in life by him, and yet there can be no doubt that, in the latter years of his life, his heart was full of love to God and his fellow-men. Camden says (*Hist. Queen Eliz.*, p. 529) that Margaret lady Derby had "a womanish curiosity" in prying into the future, "consulting with wizzards and cunning men," and hints that she aspired to the crown, her mother being the first cousin of queen

Elizabeth, and after the execution of the queen of Scots, she and James I. were in an equal degree the descendants of the two daughters of Henry VII. We know almost nothing of the history of the life of this great lady, and details are wanting to remove misapprehensions, to explain charges, and to supply motives connected with her proceedings. She had, perhaps, little of the heroic bearing of her great Plantagenet ancestors, and to turn her views to the succession, even in imagination, must have been a daring violation of her fidelity in the estimation of her lonely and unhappy maiden cousin, and not to be brooked by the contemptible spies and myrmidons with whom Elizabeth surrounded all her rivals, male and female. The chivalrous loyalty and uncompromising protestantism of lord Derby — although neither of these escaped suspicion — probably saved his wife from a catastrophe similar to that of Fotheringay and his own lands from confiscation.

The earl, like his father, appears to have been surrounded by men of various creeds and temperaments, and to have enjoyed a large share of personal popularity, and his many-sided influence vibrated throughout the county.

Mr. Crossley has pointed out to me the following pleasing reference to the earl in a MS. volume of excellent poems in his library, written at the beginning of the seventeenth century by Robert Heywood of Heywood, esq., a Lancashire gentleman, who, probably, was personally acquainted with his lordship:

> Good Henry Earle of Darby, last,
> Could ne're endure (I hear some say)
> A Suitor should come to him waste,
> And discontented goe away:
>   Ah, could we thus of CHRIST conceaue,
>   What sweet impressions would it leaue.

His will is dated 21st September 1592, and he requested that his body might be buried in his chapel at Ormskirk. Collins (Brydges' *Peerage*, vol. iii. p. 80,) states that the earl died on the 25th September 1592, but his "Funeral Certificate" will give the correct date. The countess of Derby, who seems to have attracted little public sympathy, survived her husband three years, and also her son Ferdinando, dying at Isleworth house. Dr. Goodman the dean of Westminster, wrote to Mr. Hicks on the subject of her burial in the abbey, October 22nd, 1596. (*Lansd. MS.* 83, 32.)

It will be noticed that a place was assigned her which she probably did not appreciate, nor yet appropriate, in

The Proceedings at the Funerall of HENRY EARL OF DERBY *the 4th December* 1593.

Two Conductors on Horseback, in Black Coats [? cloaks].
Then the 100 Poor Men in Gownes who went on foot from Lathom to Ormskirk.
Then 40 of the Earls Yeomen, being his Tenants.
Then the STANDARD with a Trumpeter, sounding the Dole, borne by Mr. Edward Warren.
Then the first Horse, covered wth black cloth, wth a shafferon and Escocheons, led by 2 Yeomen in Black Coats, on foot.
Then the Servants of Gentlemen and Esq^{rs} on horse back, in black Cloakes 2 and 2.
Then the Servants of Knights and Barons, on horse back, in black Cloakes.
Then the Earl of Shrewsbury Servants in Cloakes.
Then the Defuncts Servants — Retayners.
Then the Lindon borne by Mr. Edward Stanley, and a Trumpet sounding the Dole.
Then the second horse for that Earldome, covered with black cloth and Escuchions, as before.
Then the better sort of Gentlemen and Retayners, Friends, and Kindred of the defuncte, in Cloaks, on Horse-back.
Then the Earl's Chaplains, and Prebends, 2 and 2.
Then Doctors of Divinity, and Physic, and Counsellors at Law.
Then the Secretorye and other officers, the Steward, Treasurer, and Comptroller.
Then certain particular persons, and children of Kindred, with the Majors of Chester and Le'rpoole.
Then Knights and ancient Squires in Gowns.
The Bishop of Chester ye PREACHER, and had his Gentⁿ Usher and Chaplains attending him

  The Banner of Honour or GREAT BANNER borne by
   Mr. Osbaldeston.
  Then a Page on horseback, carried the Earl's guilt
   Spurr on a Staff.

The Helm and Creste borne by Somersett ⎫
The Sword and Targe by Lancaster ⎬ Herald.
The Coate of Armes by Richmond ⎭
Then the CHARIOT drawn by 4 horses with 4 Pages on their back and
a Yeoman to leade everye Horse.
  THE CORPS,
being covered wth Black Velvet, and Escochions.
Then the Horse of Estate, covered wth Black Velvet, led by the Gentⁿ
of the Horse, bare headed, on Horse-back.
The 2 Gentⁿ Ushers — one for the Earle dead, and ye other for the
Earle livinge.
  Then MR. GARTER.
Then FERDINANDO, EARLE OF DERBYE, Chiefe Mourner, riding alone
with his Hood on, and his traine borne.
Then 2 Assistants; the Earl of Shrewsburye and 7 others.
  Two Gentlemen Ushers.
Then THE COUNTESSE, and all other Ladyes in their Coaches.
  The Usher of the Hall and Chief Porter.
Then the 2 Yeomen Ushers.
Then all the Yeomen Servants, in Blacke. (*Add. MS.*, 6297, f. 264.)

   The preacher was Dr. William Chaderton, born at Nuthurst, near
Manchester, who had been at this time about fourteen years bishop of
Chester, and "always a very great friend to the house of Derby."
Preaching the funeral sermon of earl Henry "for some passages whereof
he was like to be called in question, though perhaps himself knew not
so much, I was present (says sir John Harington) when one told a
great lord [? Essex] that loved not Ferdinando the last Earle, how this
Bishop having first magnified the dead Earle for his Fidelity, Justice,
Wisdom and such Virtues as made him the best beloved man of his
rank (which praise was not altogether undeserved) he afterwards used
this apostrophe to the Earle present: 'and you (said he), noble Earle,
that not only inherit, but exceed your father's virtues, learn to keep the
love of your country as your father did. You give (said he) in your
arms, three Legs. Know you what they signify? I will tell you.
They signify three shires—CHESHIRE, DERBYSHIRE,[6] and LANCASHIRE.

---

[6] Bishop Chaderton ought to have known that the Hundred of West Derby in
Lancashire, from which the earl derived his title was not a *shire*.

Stand you fast on these three legs, and you shall fear none of their arms.'
At which this Earl a little moved, said in some heat, and not without
an oath, 'This Priest, I believe, hopes that one day I shall make him
three courtsies with my three legs.'" (Peck's *Desid. Curiosa*, vol. i.
pref. p. v. fol.; Harington's *Nugæ Antiq.* vol. ii. p. 114.) The meaning
implied seems to be that Chaderton hoped to become archbishop of
Canterbury, and the earl would do homage to him as the lord primate
of England. Chaderton was translated to Lincoln, but not to Lambeth.

R.]

WILLIAM FLEETWOOD, 1593.

MS. Vin. 92. 216 Coll. Arm.

MEMORANDⁿ Willm Fleetwood Esquire one of her Mats
Serieants at lawe sonne and heire of Robt. Fleetwood in the
Countye of Lancaster Esquire Deceassed the xxviii[th] of February
1593 whose Funerall was worshipfully solemnized the xxvii[th] of
Marche following at the pishe Churche of Great Mussenden in
Com. Buck. p Nicholas Detheck als Windeso[r] and W[m] Seager als
Somersett heraults of Armes.

Hee had to wife Marian one of the Daughters of John Boler of
Kingsey in the County of Bucks. Gent. and by her had issue sixe
sonnes and tow Daughters lyving Viz. Will[m] eldest sonne the
second Edward the third Thomas the fourthe James the fyfthe
Robt. and the sixthe Franncis Elizabeth his eldest Daughter
maried to S[r] Thomas Challoner of Stepleclaydon in Com. Buck.
Knight who hath issue by her nowe lyving three sonnes viz. Willm
Edward and Thomas and one daughter named Marye. Cordela the
second Daughter of the aforesaid Will[m] Fleetwood as yett is vnmarried.

Pedigrees of this family were entered at the Visitation of Lancaster
1613, and of Bucks in 1634 and 1669. He was reader of the Middle

Temple and recorder of the city of London, and married Marian, daughter of John Bailey of Kingsley, co. Bucks, and afterwards knighted, a pedigree of whom and other notices of his family may be found in Lipscomb's *Bucks*, vol. ii. p. 377. Robert Fleetwood, the father of the defunct, was the son of William Fleetwood of Hesketh, by Ellen, daughter of Robert Standish, a pedigree of whose descendants was recorded in Coll. Arm. in 1772, amongst whom occurs general Charles Fleetwood (called lord Fleetwood), who married Bridget, daughter of Oliver Cromwell and widow of general Ireton.

William Fleetwood is here styled an esquire, but by most authorities he is represented to have been a knight. He is sometimes stated to have been an illegitimate son.[7] His death is misstated to have taken place on 28th February 1594 in Hulton's *Penwortham*, CHETHAM series, vol. xxx. Introd. p. lv., where there is a good historical notice of his family.

William Fleetwood was of Heskin in the parish of Eccleston, and not of Hesketh in the parish of Croston, both in the county palatine.

Sir William, eldest son of the recorder, married Ann, daughter of Robert Barton of Smithills, co. Lanc., esq., and had issue four sons and six daughters. (*Lanc. MSS.*, vol. xii.)

HENRY STANLEY, 1598.

Funeral Certificate. Worden Evid.

HENRY STANLEY of Bickerstath Esquier died att his howse of Bickerstath in the Countie of Lancaster on the xxiii Julie 1598 and is buryed at Ormeskirke in the sayd Countie. He was the sonn of Sir James Stanley of Croshall in

---

[7] As regards the presumption of his illegitimacy, it appears that his arms used at his funeral were without any distinctions of illegitimacy, and were so testified by Harvey, clarencieux. Perhaps the notion of illegitimacy may have arisen from the arms of Fleetwood, annexed to his pedigree in the Visitations of Buckinghamshire, being differenced by a bordure compony argent and gules; but the bordure was frequently used simply as a mark of cadency, and had no certain signification of bastardy.

Lancashire knight and the nephieue to Thomas Erle of Derby deceassed.

He married Margarett dowter to Peter Stanley of Aughton and Bickerstath Esquier, who was the sonn to Sir William Stanley of Hooton in the Palatine of Chester knight, and by her had issewe Edward Stanley his sonn and heire now of Bickerstath, James the second sonn, and three dowters, Jane married to Gabriell Hesketh of Aughton, and Ann and Dorothie as yett vnmarried.

Ita test^r W^m ffarington.

[Henry Stanley, of Bickerstaffe, esq., was the third son of sir James and grandson of sir George Stanley, K.G., of Cross hall, knight. The father of Henry Stanley was second brother of Thomas, second earl of Derby, K.G., and Henry the third earl, in his will dated 28th August, 1572, bequeaths a legacy of 40*l.* also a piece of plate to his " cousin Henry Stanley." For a notice of the deceased see *Stanley Papers*, pt. ii. p. 96 Note. His will is abstracted and printed in *Lanc. and Chesh. Wills*, 2nd portion, p. 95. It was dated 20th July, 1598, and he mentions therein that he was "sicke in bodye." Three days after this date he died, and on the day of his death was buried, although his public funeral was not solemnized until nearly three weeks afterwards, as appears from the following entry in the *Burial Register* of Ormskirk: "1598 Auguste, Henrie Stanley of Bicarstaf Esquire, bur. xxiii^d of Julye, whose ffuneral was the 16th Auguste 1598." It is worthy of notice that the inventory of his large estate, comprised in six long vellum sheets, was written on the same day that his will is dated. It includes a great variety of chattel property at Bickerstaffe (where there was "a Domestic Chappell" and "a Chambre abouc itt"), at Cross hall, and also at Aughton hall. (*Worden Evid.*) There is a history of the Bickerstaff chantry in Ormskirk church, in the *Lanc. Chantries*, vol. i. p. 101-2, note 24. For the will of Peter Stanley, esq., father-in-law of Henry Stanley, esq., see *Lanc. and Chesh. Wills*, 2nd portion, p. 282.

The following narrative of the proceedings at the funeral of Henry Stanley, esq., is from the original in the handwriting of William ffarington of Worden, esq., comptroller of the households of Edward and

Henry, third and fourth earls of Derby, and the kinsman and executor of the deceased:

A Remembrance of the Blackes wch were cutte oute and d̃d̃. the xth of Avgvste 1598, to the Mowrners againste the tyme of the Funerall of Henry Stanley of Bickerstaffe esqwyre, viz.

ffirste to my Lo. of Derby [8]...............	iiij yards and a halfe.
To Mr Edwarde Stanley the deceassed Sone......	v yards.
To his brother James Stanley......................	v yards.
To Mr Maneringe [9]	v yards.
To M^r W^m ffarington [10]...............................	v yards.
To Mr Rawfe Worsley [11]	iiij yards.
Mrs Stanley the Widow [12]	iiij yards.
Mrs Jane Hesketh [13]..................................	iij yards and a halfe.
Mrs Anne Stanley the elder dowghter [14]	ij yards and a halfe.
Mrs Dorothe Stanley her sister [14]	ij yards and a halfe.

[8] William the sixth earl, who had succeeded his brother, earl Ferdinando, in 1594. He died in 1642.

[9] He was brother of Katherine, wife of the eldest son of the deceased. See *Stanley Papers*, pt. ii. p. 162 Note.

[10] He was the son of sir Henry ffarington of Worden, knt. His wife was Ann, daughter of sir Thomas Talbot of Bashall knt., whose mother, Ann, sister of sir Percival Hart of Lullingstone castle, in the county of Kent, knt., married sir James Stanley of Cross hall, father of the deceased. Mr. ffarington is described in the will of the deceased as his "lovinge neviewe." See his Life, *Stanley Papers*, pt. ii. Introd. and Note of sir Thomas Talbot, *ibid.* p. xxviii. note.

[11] A friend and an executor of the deceased.

[12] She was Margaret, sole child of Peter Stanley of Moore hall and Bickerstaffe, esq., by his first wife, Elizabeth, daughter and heiress of James Scarisbrick of Bickerstaffe, esq. "Mrs Elizth Stanley," her mother, was buried at Ormskirk, "Aprill xii. 1561" (*Register Book*), and her father, "Peeter Stanley of Bycarstaf" was "buryed in hys Chancell July 24, 1592." (*Ibid.*) Their daughter, "Mrs Margaret Stanley of Bicarstaff, Vid. was bur. in her owne Chappell [at Ormskirk], Nou^r 3, 1613." (*Ibid.*) She inherited Bickerstaffe and other large estates in the neighbourhood from her mother, and was the joint residuary legatee of her father.

[13] Daughter of Robert Hesketh of Rufford, esq., and of his wife, Mary, daughter of sir George Stanley of Cross hall, knt., brother of the deceased Henry Stanley.

[14] These ladies, who were sisters in half-blood, and daughters of the deceased, do not occur in the pedigree of the family. (Baines's *Lanc.* vol. iv. p. 11.) They were

Mrᵉ Katter. Stanley ¹⁵ .... iiij yards and a halfe.
Sum̃ — xlv yards and a halfe at xxijˢ the
yard amownts vnto the some of ...... 1ˡⁱ xijᵈ

To Mʳ Robert Hesketh ¹⁶............................. iiij yards.
To Mʳ Edwarde Scaresbryke ¹⁷ .... iiij yards.
To Mʳ Bartholomew Hesketh ¹⁸ .... iiij yards.
To Mʳ Gabriell Hesketh ¹⁹ .... iiij yards.
To Mʳ Edwarde Langtrye²⁰............................ iiij yards.

legatees of their father's will in 1598, but not by name. They are recorded in the following extracts from the Ormskirk *Register Books*, for which I am indebted to my worthy friend Mr. James Dixon:

"Anne Stanley, bap. December 21, 1561. Anne Stanley, virgo et generosa, bur. in her father's Chancell, July 28, 1621."

"Doretha Stanley, fil. Henrie, esq., bap. Julie 21, 1587. Dorithie Stanley, Virg., bur. Julie xxii. 1614."

[15] The second daughter of sir Randal Mainwaring of P'cover, knt., and the first wife of Edward Stanley (afterwards created a baronet), eldest son of the deceased.

[16] He was son and heir of sir Thomas Hesketh of Rufford, knt., and married Mary, daughter of sir George Stanley of Cross hall, knt., and niece of the deceased. Henry Stanley of the Crosse, esq., was named one of the executors of sir Thomas Hesketh's will in 1588. (*Stanley Papers*, pt. ii. p. 125 Note.)

[17] Grandson of Thomas Scarisbrick of Scarisbrick, esq., by his wife, Elizabeth, natural daughter of Thomas second earl of Derby. (*Stanley Papers*, pt. ii. p. 105 Note.) He had been gentleman usher to Edward third earl of Derby, 1572.

[18] See *Stanley Papers*, pt. ii. p. 124 Note.

[19] Son and heir of the preceding, and the husband of Jane Stanley, daughter of the deceased.

[20] Nephew of the deceased and son and heir of Gilbert Langtrye of Langtrye, esq., and of his wife, Ellen, daughter of sir James Stanley of Cross hall, knt. See *Stanley Papers*, pt. ii. p. 209. The family appeared at the Lancashire visitation, 1567, but not afterwards. Edward Langtree, esq., died in the year 1620, and was probably succeeded by his son, Thomas Langtree of Langtree, esq., who on the 30th April 1628 conveyed the half of the manor of Langtree, &c., to sir Ferdinando Fairfax of Denton co. York, knt., Robert Rockley of Rockley co. York, esq., William ffarington of Worden co. Lanc., esq., Henry Fairfax, rector of Ashton-under-Lyne, clerk, Thomas Worthington of Worthington, gent., and Peter Anderton of Anderton, gent., as trustees of the half of the manors of Langtree, Standish, Coppull and Worthington to the use of himself for life, afterwards to his heirs male, and failing issue, to his right heirs for ever. His estates were sequestered in June 1653 by the Commonwealth, and the owner and his family apparently ruined. (*Lanc. MSS.*, vol. xii.)

LANCASHIRE FUNERAL CERTIFICATES.

To M⁽ʳ⁾ Edwarde Svtton [21] .... iiij yards.
To M⁽ʳ⁾ Hesketh of Blackemore [22] .... iiij yards.
To M⁽ʳ⁾ Edwarde Stanley of the More Halle [23] ... iiij yards.
To M⁽ʳ⁾ Bartholomew Hesketh his wiff .... iij yards and a halfe.
To M⁽ʳˢ⁾ Rusheton the widdow [24] .... iij yards and a halfe.
To M⁽ʳˢ⁾ Margaret ffarington the widdow [25] .... iij yards and a halfe.
To Gefferey Rusheton .... iiij yards.
To his sister Anne Rusheton .... iij yards and a halfe.
    Sum — l⁽ᵗⁱᵉ⁾ yards at xvj⁽ˢ⁾ the yard amovnts
    vnto the some of .... xl⁽ˡⁱ⁾

To M⁽ʳ⁾ Ric. Aughton................................... iiij yards.

[21] William Sutton, esq., married Margaret, daughter of Thomas Stanley, second baron Monteagle, and Alice and Margaret Sutton, sisters, were legatees of Peter Stanley, esq., in 1589. Mrs. Sutton married, secondly, John Talbot, esq.

[22] Thomas, son of sir Thomas Hesketh of Rufford, had lands at Blackmore, in Maudesley, in the parish of Croston, under his father's will, 20th June 1588. (*Lanc. and Chesh. Wills.*)

[23] Moor hall, in Aughton, near Ormskirk, is just on the border of the township of Bickerstaffe. (Baines's *Lanc.* vol. iv. p. 228.) He was the son of Peter Stanley, esq., by his second wife, Ciceley Ireland, and half brother of Margaret, wife of the deceased. There is an ancient stone tablet over the entrance to Moor hall, on which the following record is inscribed:

    "PETER STANLEY ESQVIR
    AND CECELEY HYS WIF.
    1566."

[24] She was Ann, sister of the deceased, daughter of sir James Stanley of Cross hall, and the third wife and now widow of captain Ralph Rushton of Pontalgh. Her life was almost as chequered as that of her worthless husband, who was a type of a somewhat large class, notwithstanding all the glowing eulogies and poetical embellishments which have been lavished upon chivalry. This ill-used lady, having survived all her children, was living in Ormskirk, 17th March 1611-12, and was then aged 80 years, and in the full possession of her memory and other faculties. (*Lanc. MSS.*) Geoffrey and Ann Rushton were not her children, but probably were the children of her husband's cousin, John Rushton of Dunkenhalgh, esq., who married Alice, daughter of sir James Stanley of Cross hall, and whose grandmother, Ann, wife of Richard Rushton esq., was a Talbot of Samlesbury. (*Lanc. MSS.* vol. xii.)

[25] She was the widow of Henry ffarington, gent., second son of William ffarington, esq., the nephew (by marriage) of the deceased, and daughter and heiress of Edward Browster of Macclesfield, esq. Her husband died a young man.

34   LANCASHIRE FUNERAL CERTIFICATES.

To Mr Wm Stanley brother of Mr Stanley of the
   More Halle .... iiij yards.
Mrs Aughton .... iij yards and a halfe.
ffor ix Lyvery Cottes .... xiij yards and a halfe.
It. for a Gowne to one of the Wating women ... iij yards and a halfe.
   Suṁ — xxviij yards and a halfe at xj^s vj^d
   the yarde amownts vnto .... xvj^{li} vij^s ix^d

It. for xi Lyvercy cottes more cōteyning xvi yards
   and three qvart^{9}s at x^s the yard amowuteth
   vnto the some of .... viij^{li} vij^s vi^d
        Suṁ — viij^{li} vij^s vj^d
            Suṁ totall —- Cxiiij^{li} xvj^s iij^d

It. rec. also of Blacke fryse for to make pore
   mens gownes of, xxx^{tie} yards at xvij^d the
   yarde .... xlij^s vi^d
        Suṁ ... xlij^s vj^d

   A note lykewise of other Clothe as yet to be pvided for for
   the licke vse, viz. at xvj^s the yarde.

ffirste for Mrs Anne ffarington, wife of the said
   W^m ffarington .... iij yards and a halfe
                                           and halfe a quarter.
ffor Mrs Langtrye............................ iij yards and a halfe.
ffor Mrs Sutton ... . iij yards and a halfe.
ffor Mrs Stanley of the More Halle........... iij yards and a halfe.
ffor Mrs Alice Sytton .... ij yards and a halfe.
        Suṁ — xvi yards and a half and half
            a quart^r .... xiij^{li} j^s
            Suṁ ... xiij^{li} j^s

It. ffor a Gowne to a wating Made .... iij yards and a halfe
                                            at xj^s vj^d the yarde.
        Suṁ — iij yards and a halfe
            Suṁ .... xl^s iij^d

LANCASHIRE FUNERAL CERTIFICATES. 35

It. for a fote cloth to the sayd Mr Edwarde Stanley the Chieffe Mowrnor ....
It. xvj yardes of Blacke cotton for covering of
the Hearse, at x^d the yarde .... xiiij^s iiij^d
      Sum̃ ... xiiij^s iiij^d
        Sum̃ TOTALL is Cxxxij^{li} xviij^s iiij^d
     wherof payd the xth Avgvste 1598,
     in parte of payment the some of l^{li}
Memd. that there is owing also vnto the sayd
Roger Langton for sertaine stuffe solde vnto
my Cossin Edward Stanley, as appereth by
a Bylle of psells, the some of .... iij^{li} ix^s

   The names of the S'vantes of the sayd Henry Stanley vnto
   whom mowrnyng cottes were giuen againste the ffunerall
   of the sayd Mr Stanley, viz.

Robert Leadebeatter	Adam Chadwicke
Petter Charlles	T^o Cobõne
Rodger Wallworth	Phillippe Holme
Rye. Wilkinson	Jhon ffogg
James Chadwicke	T^o Hunter
T^o Waring	Henry Lathom
Petter Leadbeatter	Jhon Lyon
T^o Seffeton	Edwarde Som̃re
Gabryell Mason	Symon Smyth
Jhon Davisst	Wm Wadington *R.*]

MRS. MARGARET RADCLIFF, 1599.

Funeral Certificates, I. 16. 60. *Coll. Arm.*

MRS. Margrett Radcliff one of the Maides of honor to her Matie daughtor to Sr John Radcliffe knight of Wordsall in the Countie of Lancastr: departed this mortall Lyffe at Richmond, in the Countie of Surrey (the Court beinge then theire) the xth of

November 1599 whose ffunerall was worshipfully solempnised at the parishe church of St Margaretts in Westminster the 22 daye of the same moneth. The pennon borne by Mr Barton of Smythells, Mrs Anne Russell chife morner, beinge ledd by Sr John Radcliffe Knight, Brother to the defunct. And the assistantes were the Lady Walsinghã, Mrs Radcliffe M^rs ffitton, Mrs Carey, Mrs Aunslowe, and M^rs wyngfeld Mr. Clarencieulx and Rouge Dragon attending at the said ffuncrall her ma^ties will and pleasure was, that this gentilwoman should be Buried as a lady. The whiche was accomplished in manner and forme aforsaid the day and yere aboue written.

Will^M Camden Clarenceux
W^M Smith, Rouge Dragon.

[Margaret Radcliffe, eldest daughter of sir John Radcliffe of Ordsall, knt., M.P., (buried in the choir of Manchester collegiate church on the 11th February 1589-90, aged 53) was baptised at Manchester on the 6th March 1573-4. She had by her father's will a share in lands in Lincolnshire, Derbyshire and Rochdale, during her life, and a legacy of one thousand marks. (*Stanley Papers*, pt. ii. p. 172 Note.) She was the eldest daughter of her parents, and seems to have been introduced at court, at an early period of her life, probably through the great interest of the Derby family, with whose household her father had been connected. It is recorded that at the court "she became the favourite maid of honour to queen Elizabeth" (*Lanc. MSS.* vol. xii. p. 198), a statement corroborated by the text, and probably founded upon it. She is also recorded to have "died of grief for the loss of her brothers" (*ibid.*), her second brother, William (baptised at Manchester on the 28th June 1577), having been killed, in 1598, at Blackwater in Ireland, at the early age of 20, whilst fighting against Hugh earl of Tyrone; and her elder brother, sir Alexander (baptised at Manchester on the 28th January 1571-2), having been also slain in Ireland, at the age of 27, in 1599. (*Ibid.*) She had five brothers, all of whom were distinguished by their military bravery; and whilst it is recorded that three of them died in battle, the probability is that the other two, who were twins, also fell in the same field. There is nothing surprising in the fact that the queen, always sparing of her honours, should have commanded the sister of these brave and gallant soldiers to be buried according to her birth "as a lady." The text can scarcely be meant to imply that the queen had conferred rank or title upon her.

Mrs. Anne Russell and the other ladies styled "Mistress" were maids of honour, or young ladies of the court. The only relatives present at the funeral were sir John Radcliffe and Mr. Barton of Smithills, although the mother of the deceased long survived the death of her daughter. There is a pedigree of the Radcliffes of Ordsall, commencing with Robert Radcliffe of Ordsall, sheriff of Lancashire 14 Edw. III., and brought down to sir William Radcliffe, living 5 Edw. VI., in *Lanc. MSS.* vol. xii. And a very elaborate genealogical history of the same great house, deduced by William Radcliffe, esq., rouge croix, in *Lanc. MSS.* vol. xiii. *R.*]

KATHERINE BRETARGH, 1601.

Lansdowne MS. 879, *fo.* 7.

KATHERINE late wief of Willm Bretterghe of Brettersholt in the Countie of Lancaster Gentleman deceassed the last daie of Maye Anno Dñi 1601.

The said Katherine was daughter of John Bruyn of Bruyn Stapleforde in the County of Chester Esquir who hath issue by the said Willm one onelie daughter named Anne. The said defunct in respecte of the Famylie wherof shee is discended did beare in one four scuerall Coates of Armes in such sorte as the same is above marshalled.

    The firste per le nosme de Bruyn
    The Soconde per le nosme de Praers
    The Thirdd per le nosme de Greenewaye
    The fourthe per le nosme de Dedwoode.

The Bretterghs of Brettergh-holt recorded a pedigree at the Visitation of Lancashire in 1664-5. The above-named William Brettergh died about the year 1616. He was son of William Brettergh of Bretterghsholt (who was living in 1596), by Maude, daughter of Thomas Chisenhall of Chisenhall, co. Lanc. Katherine the defunct was the first wife of William, and had issue by him an only child, Anne, who married Gilbert Gerard of Crew Wood, co. Chester. The said William married, secondly, Anne, daughter of William Hyde of Urmstone, co. Lanc., esq., by whom he had issue, Nathaniel Brettergh of Bretterghsholt, who died in 1659, having married Katherine, daughter of Edward Smith of Knowsley, co. Lanc., by whom he had issue, James, oldest son, aged 38 in 1664; and who married Deborah, daughter of John Bushell of Mickledale, in Cheshire; William, second son of Nathaniel, who married Anne Glove of Warrington, co. Lanc.; and three daughters, 1. Anne, wife of Christopher Powell; 2. Dorothy, wife of Nathan Lowe; 3. Katherine. William Bretterghe, by his second wife (Ann Hyde), had also two daughters; 1. Catherine, wife of Edward Stockley of Prescot, co. Lanc.; 2. Elizabeth, wife of William Hatton, M.D. James Brettergh above mentioned, by Deborah Bushell his wife, had issue, 1. Jonathan, aged eight in 1664; 2. Edward; and six daughters, viz.: Anne, Mary, Deborah, Elizabeth, Catherine and Phœbe. (*Coll. Arms*, London.)

[There is a pedigree of the family in *Lanc. MSS.* vol. xii., commencing with William Brettergh, who lived in the time of Edw. I., and brought down to Dugdale's *Visitation of Lancashire*. The lady, whose death is here recorded, was remarkable for her piety and good works, and her funeral sermons and life were published. The former with the titles: "*Death's Advantages Little Regarded,*" and "*The Soules Solace against Sorrow*, preached in two funerall Sermons at Childwall in Lancashire, at the buriall of Mistris Katherin Brettergh, the third of June 1601. The one by William Harrison, one of the Preachers appointed by Her Maiestie for the Countie Palatine of Lancaster; the other by William Leygh, Bachelor of Diuinity and Pastor of Standish. Whereunto is annexed, *The Christian Life and godly death of the said Gentlewoman*. The second edition, corrected and amended." London, 12mo, 1612. The first sermon was preached from Isaiah lvii. 1, and there is "An Epistle to the Christian Reader," by Mr. Harrison, pp. 4. The sermon extends to pp. 84. The second sermon was preached from Isaiah lvii. 2, and there is an epistle "To the Reverend man of God and faithful Preacher, Mr. William Leygh, B.D. and Pastor of Standish in Lancashire, [from] William Brettergh, [who] wisheth encrease of all good graces for the gathering of Gods saints and building vp of his Church, and for his owne euerlasting salvation in Jesus Christ. Dated London, 20 November 1601." It appears that Mr. Brettergh, after much entreaty, obtained a copy of the sermon from Mr. Leigh, and published it without his authority, "rather than venture upon earthly replies, and so hazard the want of so heavenly a solace for God's children." The sermon extends to pp. 77, and contains many eloquent and touching passages, and is a fine specimen of pulpit oratory of the puritan school of theology. The life is entitled "*A Brief Discovrse of the Christian Life and Death of Mistris Katherin Brettergh, late wife of Master William Brettergh of Bretterghoult, in the Countie of Lancaster, Gentleman,* who departed this world the last of May 1601. With the manner of a bitter conflict she had with Satan, and blessed conquest by Christ, before her death, to the great glorie of God, and comfort of all Beholders. Micah 7. 8; Psalm 37. 37. 12mo, London, Imprinted by Felix Kyngston." The life is preceded by "An Epistle to the Christian Reader;" also, "A Postscript to Papists," and three copies of elegiac verses on her death, as well as the following lines by W. F.:

Katherina { Pura, Christo quàm purgata,
Vita, Christo præparata,
Morte, Christo dedicata,
Cœlis, Christo coniugata.

The life extends to pp. 38. The relatives and friends who visited her during her sickness were her brother, the famous John Bruen of Bruen Stapleford, esq., William Fox of Rhodes, near Manchester, William and John Brettergh, William Woodward of Shevington, John Holland, Mrs. Maud Brettergh, Mrs. Scholastica Fox, Mr. Edward Aspinwall (who wrote verses on her death), Elizabeth Challoner, Richard Orme, John Wrightington, esq., Raphe Heaton, and Mr. Harrison the preacher.

She was married when about 20 years old to Mr. Brettergh, a young man of ancient family, and died of a fever about two years afterwards, having had issue only one daughter, Anna Brettergh. Her biographer informs us that "she came from the habitation of *Abraham* to dwell in *Sodome* amidst the tents of *Kedar*, that is to say, among inhumane bands of brutish Papists, induring many temporal grievances from them, yet her knowledge, patience, mild inclination and constancie for the truth was such as that her husband was farther builded up in Religion by her meanes, and his face dailie more and more hardened against the diuell and all his plaguie agents, the *Popish Recusants, Church Papists, prophane Atheists* and *carnall Protestants*, which swarmed together like Hornets in those parts,"—near Liverpool. The biographer concludes his well-written life by recording that "her Funerall was accomplished at Childwall Church on Wednesday following [she died on Whitsunday, 31st May], being the third of June 1601;" and he adds: "Now for conclusion, seeing this blessed Gentlewoman is taken from among vs, and received into the holy habitations of the heauenlie Jerusalem, there to remaine in ioy, glory and blessedness for euermore, let vs lament for our losse, but reioyce for her gaine, and let vs pray, that in heart wee could as willinglie wish to be with her as she is now vnwilling to be with us. Solomon saith: The memorie of the iust shall be blessed, but the name of the wicked shall not. Prov. x. 7."

It is not stated by whom the life was written, but there is internal evidence to lead to the conclusion that the author was the Rev. William Hinde, B.D., who wrote the interesting life of John Bruen of Bruen Stapleford, esq. His wife was the sister of Mrs. Bruen, but neither of them are named in Mrs. Brettergh's life. *R.*]

SIR EDWARD STANLEY, 1604.

Lansdowne MS. 879, *fo.* 31.

SIR Edward Stanley Knight dyed at Lathom in Lancashire on the vii[th] of August 1604 and lyeth buryed in Ormes church within the said County.

He was third sonne to Edward Earl of Darby, Lord Stanley, Strange, Lord of Man, and Knight of the Garter &c. he dyed vpon the day aforesaid and was never married.

He was third son of Edward third earl of Derby, K.G., by Dorothy his first wife, daughter of Thomas Howard duke of Norfolk; and was of Eynsham, co. Oxford. *K.*
["September 4. 1604. Sere Edward Stanley bur. in my Lords Chaple." (Ormskirk *Register of Burials.*) In the elaborate pedigree of the house of Stanley in Baines's *Hist. of Lanc.* vol. iv. he is erroneously said to have died in 1590. *R.*]

EDWARD NORRES, 1606.

Harl. MS. 2041, *Book of Funerals in Cheshire, Lancashire, and North Wales, by Richard St. George, Norroy,*

EDWARD Norres of Speake in the Countie of Lanckester Esqre dyed one the one and twenteth of May 1606 and lyeth interred in the parishe church of Childwall in the said Countie.

He married Margerett one of the daughters and heyres of Robt. Smalwood of the City of Westminster Esqr they have yssue Sr William Norres, Knight of the honorable order of the Bathe, their sonne and heire; who hath maried Dame Elinor sole daughter to William Molyneux Esqr, sonne and heire of Sr Richard Molyneux of Sefton in the said Countie of Lanc. Knight.

The said Sr William Norres Knight and Dame Elinor have yssue Edward Norres Esqr sonne and heire apparent, William Norres second sonne, Allen Norres third sonne, Thomas Norres fourth sonne, Richard Norres fift sonne, Alexander Norres sixt sonne, and Henrie seventh sonne.

Margaret Norres eldest Daughter[26] of the said Sr William and Dame Elinor, Bridget second daughter,[27] Elizabeth third daughter, and Ann fourth Daughter.

Edward Norres second sonne of Edward and Margrett.

Anne eldest daughter to the said Edward and Margrett, first

---

[26] Second daughter. *(Ormerod).*   [27] Eldest daughter. *(Ibid).*

married to Sr Thomas Butler of Bewsey in the Countie Lanc.
Knight; the have no yssue. To her second husband she maried
Phillip Draycort, sonne and heire of John Dracort of Pensley[28] in
the Countie Stafford Esqr; they have yssue, Edward Dracort,
Margeret and Ann Dracorte.

Marye second daughter of Edward and Margerett maried Thomas Clifton of Westbye in the Countie Lanc. Esqr; they have
yssue, Cutberd Clifton their sonne and heire, who hath maried
Ann daughter of Christopher Tylsley of Morley in the Countie
Lanc. Esqr; they have yssue Tho. Clifton.

Margrett third daughter of Edward and Margerett, maried Edw.
Tarbock sonne and heire apparent of Edw. Tarbock of Tarbock in
the Countie of Lanc. Esqr; they have yssue Edw. Tarbock their
sonne and heire, George second sonne, Willm third sonne, Elionor
eldest daughter, and Margrett Tarbock second daughter.

Emilia fourth daughter of Edw. and Margrett, maried Willm
Blundell of Crosbie in the countie of Lanc. Esqr; they have yssue
Nichol, Ann and Margrett Blundell.

Winifred fift daughter, maried Ric. Banester of Wem in the
Coutie of Salop Esqr; they had yssue but all died younge.

Martha[29] sixt Daughter, first maried to Thurstan Anderton, heire
vnto his brother James Anderton of Lostock in the Countie of
Lanc. Esqr; they had yssue but none nowe livinge. To her second
husband, she maried Sr Henry Bunbery of Stanney in the Countie
of Chester Knight; they have yssue John, Tho. Anne and Elioner
Bunbery.

Perpetua seventh[30] daughter of Edw. and Mar. maried to Tho.
Westbie, Brother and heire to Jo. Westbie of Mowbrick in the
Countie of Lanc. Esqr.

[28] Payusley.
[29] In the pedigree of the family (*Lanc. MSS.* vol. xii.) she is called "Agatha."
[30] In the pedigree in the Visitation of the county of Lancaster, 1664, and also in Ormerod's *Memoir*, she is recorded as being the *eldest* daughter.

LANCASHIRE FUNERAL CERTIFICATES.

In the *Topographer and Genealogist*, vol. ii. pp. 357–383, is an account and copy of a " Genealogical declaration respecting the Family of Norres, written by Sir William Norres of Speke, co. Lancaster, in the year 1563; accompanied by an abstract of ancient charters." The document here alluded to, which is copied from the *Harl. MSS.* 1997, appears to have escaped the notice of Mr. Baines, sen., the historian of Lancashire. It appears, however, that much reliance cannot be placed upon sir William's statements concerning his ancestors. The abstracts from charters extend from the reign of Henry III. to that of Elizabeth.

In the Visitation of co. Lanc. anno 1567, the pedigree of Norres of Speke was registered but *not* certified by sir William, as stated in *Top. and Gen.* He was father of Edward Speke, the subject of this funeral certificate. The pedigree is extensively given in *Baines*, vol. iii. p. 754, and *Gregson*, p. 204. The descendants of Edward have never recorded their pedigree in Coll. Arms. That entered by Mr. Lodge in 1808, of Norres of Davyhulme near Manchester, is a junior branch, and they bore three bezants on the fess in their arms; the family being now represented by Robert H. Norres, esq., of Davyhulme hall. *K.*

[A MEMOIR of the Lancashire house of Le Noreis or Norres and its Speke branch in particular, with notices of its connexion with military transactions at Flodden, Edinburgh and Musselburgh, was read in April 1850, at a meeting of the Historic Society of Lancashire and Cheshire, and having been printed in the second volume of their proceedings, was afterwards privately printed, with additions by the author, George Ormerod, esq., D.C.L., F.R.S., F.S.A., of Tyldesley and Sedbury park. Liverpool, 8vo, 1850, pp. 55. The Table of Contents is as follows:

Introductory Remarks.
I. 1. Settlement of Le Noreis in Blackrod in the time of Richard I.
   2. Account of the Blackrod line of Le Noreis.
   3. Le Noreis or Norreys of Sutton and Daresbury, from whom the Speke line is deduced.
   4. Examination of the Evidence illustrating the connection of the Sutton and Speke line of Norres.
   5. Norres or le Norcis of Speke, previous to their connexion with Erneys of Sefton and Speke.

II. 1. Descent of the manor of Speke from Gernet to Norres through Molyneux of Sefton and Erneys.

2. Deduction of representation in blood, as derived from Gernet by Norres through Molyneux of Crosby and Erneys.

III. Collateral male lines of Speke.
   1. Norres of Park Hall in Blackrod.
   2. —— of West Derby (second line).
   3. —— of Fyfield in Berks.
   4. —— of West Derby (third line).
   5. —— of Middleforth and Davyhulme.
   6. —— of Bolton.
   7. —— *alias* Robinson, bishop of Bangor.
   8. —— of Orford, and the lines of Norres stated to have adopted the local names of Halsned, Hardieshaw, Eltonhead, &c.
   9. Norreys, earl of Berkshire.

IV. Continuation of the Speke line from the alliance with Erneys to the determination of the direct male line.

The descents previous to Henry Norres, the husband of Clemence Harrington.

Henry Norres of Speke and Blackrod, and examination of the legend which confounded him with an imaginary sir Edward Norres.

Services of Lancashire and Cheshire knights and gentry at Flodden.

Brasses of Henry and Clemence Norres at Childwall church.

Biographical notice of sir William Norres, and notice of his connexion with the transactions at Edinburgh and Musselburgh, and the death of his son at the latter.

Notice of Edward Norres, son of sir William.

ILLUSTRATIONS OF THE PRECEDING MEMOIR.

I. Authorities for the several statements.
II. Records relative to the possession of Blackrod by Hugh le Norres.
III. Extracts from the "Declaration" of sir William Norres, relative to his representation of the Blackrod line of Norres.
IV. Descent of Le Noreis as given in the Visitation of 1567.
V. Probable origin of the arms of Norres.
VI. Charter of Henry le Noreis, recognizing his brothers, who are considered identical with the founders of the Speke line.
VII. Documents relative to the grant of the Haselwal interest in Speke to the Norres family.
VIII. Lancashire Deeds witnessed by Allan, Robert, and John le Noreis, considered to be the brothers of Henry le Noreis above mentioned.
IX. Former memorials of Norres at Childwall.
X. Notice of Discussions on the Wainscot at Speke.

XI.	Extract from the Speke Pedigree proving the presence of the several brothers of the Speke family at Flodden.
XII.	Brasses in Childwall church.
XIII.	Autograph Inscription by sir William Norres in the books brought from Edinburgh as trophies.
XIV.	Extract from Holinshed relative to the death of sir William Norres in the battle of Musselburgh.
XV.	Notice of the Banner of Boswell taken by sir William Norres at Musselburgh.
XVI.	Inscription attached to the carved mantlepiece in the great parlour at Speke.
XVII.	Notices of the part taken by Norres of Speke and other Lancashire branches of that house in the war between king Charles I. and the parliament. Plates and Pedigrees. *R.*]

SIR ALEXANDER BARLOWE, 1620.

Funeral Certif. I. 22.   33^b *Coll. Arm.*

Sr Alexander Barlowe in ye County of Lancaster knight, departed this lyfe the 20 of Aprill, and was buried in ye Collegiatt Churche of Manchester, being of the age of 63 yeares when he dyed. He maried Mary 2^d Dā of Sr Urion Brerton of Handford in ye County of Chest. knight, and by her had issue 8 sonnes and 6 daughters, vizt Alexander eldest sonne and heire, who together with his father was knighted at ye Coronaĉon of King James, and doth succeede his father in all his possessions, Lands and tenements and hereditament of Barlowe and elsewhere; George 2^d sonne of the defunct, William 3rd sonne, Edward 4th sonne, John 5 sonne, Robert 6 sonne dyed an infant, Edmund 7 sonne, and Robert 8 sonne now living. His daughters were Elizabeth, first dā dyed an infant, Margret 2^d dā maried to Sr John Talbot of Salebury in Com. Lancaster knight, ffrancys 3 dā, Mary 4th dā, Jane 5 and Catharine 6 daughter. This Sr Alexander Barlow now living maried first Elizabeth 2^d dā of Edward Lo. Morley, and by her hath issue one sonne and 2 daught. Secondly he maried Dorothy 3rd dā of Sr Thomas Greasley of Draklow in ye County of Derby, and by her hath one sonne. This

Certificat was taken the 30 of October 1620 by Leonard Smetheley Deputy for y⁰ Office of Armes, being truely given by Sʳ Alexander Barlow and testified by yᵉ subscription of his name.

From the pedigree entered at the Visitation of 1664 it appears that he was the son of Alexander Barlow of Barlow, by Elizabeth daūr and coheir of George Leigh, brother of Thomas Leigh of High Leigh, co. Cest., and grandson of Ellis Barlow of Barlow,[31] by Anne daūr of Oates Reddish of Reddish, co. Lanc. The only issue mentioned of the defunct in the Visitation are sir Alexander, who ob. 1642, and Margaret above mentioned. The issue of sir Alexander the son, by his 1ˢᵗ wife, were Alexander, who ob. s.p. about 1654, having marrᵈ Frances oldest daūr of William Brereton of Ashley, co. Cest.; Catherine, wife of Henry Norris of West Derby; and Dorothy, wife of [James] Gossach[32] of Gossach, co. Lanc. By his 2ᵈ wife, Dorothy Gresley, he had Thomas of Barlow, aged 46 in 1664, who marrᵈ Winifred, eldest daūr of Anthony Meynell of North Kilvington, co. York, esq., by whom, Thomas, Alexander, Anthony and Mary. His daūrs by the said Dorothy were Anne, a nun of St. Clare; Mary, wife of Caryl viscount Molineux; and Elizabeth, wife of Thomas Vavasour of Weston, co. York, esq. *K.*

[Sir Alexander Barlow was aged twenty-six 27 Elizabeth (1584); at the death of his father received knighthood from James I. at Whitehall in 1603; was contracted in the face of the Church, at Middleton in the county of Lancaster, September 22, 1562, to Elizabeth, daughter and coheir of Ralph Belfield of Clegg hall, near Rochdale, gent., but the marriage does not appear to have been consummated, and he obtained a divorce from the consistory court of Chester on the 21st October 1574. (*Lanc. MSS.*, vol. xii., Barlow; *Stanley Papers*, pt. ii. p. 211, note, CHETHAM series.) He married, secondly, Mary, daughter of sir Urian Brereton of Honford, in the county of Chester, knt., by whom he had issue. His will is dated April 14th 1617, and he was buried by torch light in the Collegiate church of Manchester on the 21st April 1620, as "sir Alexander Barlow the elder knt.;" dying, as he expresses himself in his will, "a true and pfecte recusante Catholicke."

---

[31] Ellis Barlowe was eldest son of Roger Barlow, son and heir of sir Alexander Barlowe, who commences the pedigree at the Visitation of 1597.   [32] Gorsuch.

For a view of Barlow hall, a pedigree of the family, and much interesting documentary information, see Booker's *History of Chorlton Chapel*, CHETHAM series, vol. xlii. pp. 249 *et seq.*; and for a notice of sir Alex. Barlow, *Stanley Papers*, pt. ii. p. 210, note, CHETHAM series; where on p. 212, for sir *William* read *Urian* Brereton, and for 1624 read 1620. *R.*]

SIR EDMUND TRAFFORD, 1620.

Funeral Certif. I. 22.   53^b *Coll. Arm.*

SIR Edmund Trafford of Trafford in Com. Lancast knight, departed this life the 19 of May 1620, and was buried the 28 of the same month in the Collegiatt Churche of Manchester, when he had lived 59 yeares. He first maried Margrett dā and coheire of John Bouth of Barton in ye County aforesaid Esq., by whom he had issue one daughter and three sonnes viz. Edmund eldest sonne disinherited, John 2^d sonne, Richard 3^d sonne, and Elizabeth his daughter.

He married to his 2^d wife the Lady Mildred dā of Thomas Cecill Earle of Excester, by whom he had issue Cecilia a daughter, and Cecill a sonne, knighted in his fathers lyfe tyme, whome his father made heire of all his land and sole Executor, who now doth succeede him in ye possession and occupation of all his lands demeasnes Parkes and priviledges and whatsoever his late father did hold given vnto him by his father and confirmed vnto him by his eldest brother Edmund and the rest, under their handes and seale, he paying unto his said elder brother and sister Elizabeth such porcōns and anuuities as is agreed vpon, and soe to continew heire and successor to his father, both he and his heires to be "Trafford of Trafford." This Certificat was taken by Leonard Smetheley, Deputy to the Office of Armes for ye county of Lancaster, the 31 of October 1620, and testified to be true by ye subscription of the sayd Sr Cecill Trafford.

Sir Edmund Trafford was the son of sir Edmund Trafford of Trafford knt. by Elizabeth his second wife, daur. of sir Ralph Leicester of Tofte, co. Chester, kn¹, and grandson of sir Edmund Trafford of Trafford knt. by Anne dau'r of sir Alexander Radclyffe of Ordsall kn¹, as appears by the Visitations of co. Lanc. 1613 and 1664. The children of the deceased by his first wife were Elizabeth, wife of Richard Fleetwood of Penwortham, co. Lanc. gent. 1. Edmund, who married but died without issue, 2. John, and 3. Richard; both died unmarried. By his second wife he had issue sir Cecil Trafford knt., aged 65 in 1664, who marr⁴ Penelope, dau'r of sir Humphrey Davenport of Sutton, co. Chester, knt., lord chief baron of the exchequer, by whom he had issue, 1. Edmund, aged 39 in 1664, who mar⁴ Frances dau' of Philip Draycote of Paynesley, co. Stafford, esq.; 2. Cecill; 3. Humphrey; 4. John of Croston, co. Lanc., aged 30 in 1664, and who mar⁴ Anne da' and coheir of Richard Ashton of Croston, esq^re [by whom Cecil aged 2, Ashton who died young, and John, ancestor of the present baronet]; 5. Henry, ob. unmar⁴; 6. William; and two daurs. 1. Penelope wife of John Downes of Wordley, co. Lanc., esq.; 2. Mildred wife of William Massey of Puddington, co. Cest., esq^r.

From sir Cecil Trafford, who mar⁴ Penelope Davenport, a pedigree was recorded in Coll. Arms in 1842 of their descendants, one of whom, sir Thomas Joseph Trafford, baronet, was so created in 1841; and by royal licence in the same year took the surname of De Trafford, the ancient patronymic of the family. *K.*

[It does not appear to be known why Edmund, the eldest son of sir Edmund Trafford, knt., was disinherited. He was married, although the name of his wife is not recorded, and in the family pedigree he is said to have had no issue. The large estates of the Booths of Barton passed away from the blood and lineage of that great house on or before the death of Edmund Trafford and his two brothers (maternal grandsons of John Booth, esq.), and were confirmed by deed to Cecil Trafford, their brother in half blood, in whose collateral descendants they are still vested. For a notice of sir Edmund Trafford, knt., whose funeral certificate is here printed, see *Stanley Papers*, pt. ii. p. 99, note, CHETHAM series; and for an extensive pedigree of the family, Baines's *History of Lancashire*, vol. iii. p. 111; and for abtracts of the evidences of the Booths and Traffords, *Lanc. MSS.* vol. xxv. *R.*]

SIR THOMAS IRELAND, 1625.

Original Funeral Certificates of the North in Coll. Arm., No. 4.

SIR Thomas Ireland of Beusey in the County of Lancaster K[t] departed this mortall life at Beusey the 17 day of July 1625, interred in Warrington Church in y[e] sayde County in Butlers chappell, beinge then his own chappell.

The sayd defunct marryed Margaret daughter of Sir Thomas Aston of Aston in the county of Chester K[t] and by her hadd issue, Thomas Ireland sonne and heire unto the defunct being then of the age of 23 yeares att the time of his fathers deathe then vnmarryed since upon the takinge of this Certificate marryed vnto Margaret daughter vnto Sir Thomas Standley of Auderley K[t] defuncte, by whom hee had issue, Thomas which dyed younge and Margaret now of y[e] age of 7 yeares and a halfe or thereabouts.

Robert the 2nd Sonne vnto the defuncte vnmarryed.

Elizabeth the eldest daughter of the defuncte marryed William Banckes of Winstanley Esq[r] by whom she had issue James Banckes and Thomas Banckes and William Bancks.

Ellinor the 2nd daughter vnto the defuncte marryed John Atherton of Atherton Esq[r] by whom shee had George and John wth others since.

Margaret the youngest daughter vnto the defuncte marryed John Jefferyes of Acton in the County of Denby Esq[r] by whom he hath issue Margaret and John.

The sayd defuncte marryed afterwards Suzane daughter of Sir Thomas Cheek K[t] by whom hee had noe issue.

The sayd defuncte marryed afterwards Margaret daughter vnto William Lloyde of Halton Esq[r] and widdowe of John Jefferyes of Acton Esq. by whom hee had noe issue.

This Certificate was taken at Beusey vpon the 15th day of January 1637 by Randle Hoolme of the Citty of Chester deputy to the office of Armes and testified vnder the hande of Thomas Ireland of Bensey Esq. sonne and heire of the sayd defuncte.

THOMAS IRELAND.

[It will be observed that this funeral certificate was not issued at the time of Mr. Ireland's death, but was the result of an inquiry made twelve years afterwards, probably at the instigation of the heralds, by the elder Randle Holme of Chester.

The defunct was the second son of Robert Ireland, gent. (a younger son of Ireland of Lydiate) by his wife, Margaret, daughter of Richard Fox of Broughton, in the county palatine of Chester. (*Lanc. MSS.*, vol. iii. p. 314.) There is no pedigree of sir Thomas Ireland in the *Lancashire Visitations*. He adopted the legal profession, and had been successful at the bar, as he was appointed vice-chamberlain of the city and county of Chester, and purchased before the year 1586 the Bewsey estate, including the manor and advowson of the rectory of Warrington, of Edward Butler, esq. (Marsh's *Hist. of Boteler's Free Grammar School*, p. 68.) He was knighted at Bewsey by James I. on the 21st August 1617. He bore six quarterings, differenced by a crescent upon a crescent.

The facts contained in this certificate being authenticated by the son of sir Thomas may be presumed to be accurate, but they differ in some respects from the pedigree of the family deduced in the year 1676 by captain Booth of Stockport. (*Lanc. MSS.*, vol. iii. p. 313.) Sir Thomas Ireland is there stated to have had by his first wife (whose name is omitted) an eldest son George, who was his heir apparent, but who died 8th Charles I. 1633 without issue male, leaving by his wife the widow of —— Banastre of Bank, a sole child, Margaret Ireland, who became the wife of Cuthbert Clifton of Southworth, in the county of Lancaster, esq., brother of sir Thomas Clifton of Clifton and Westby, bart., by whom she had no issue. Sir Thomas Ireland married secondly, Margaret, daughter of sir Thomas Aston of Aston, knt., and had issue, 1. Baldwin, who died young; 2. Thomas, "to whom his father gave Bewsey," and who endorsed this funeral certificate; 3. Robert, who died unmarried. Sir Thomas's daughters were, 1. Elizabeth, married William, son and heir of James Bankes of Winstanley, esq.; 2. Eleanor, married John Atherton of Atherton, esq.; 3. Bridget, married Henry Byrom of Byrom, esq.; 4. Margaret (omitted by captain Booth), married John Jefferys of Acton in the county of Denbigh, esq., and became the mother of the notorious judge Jefferys, created baron of Wem, in the county of Salop, who is now represented (through the earls of Pomfret) by sir Thomas Hesketh of Rufford, bart., M.P.

After the death of his wife Margaret Aston, sir Thomas was twice married, according to this certificate, but both marriages are omitted by captain Booth. Neither is it recorded, as it might have been, in this certificate, that Margaret, widow of sir Thomas, became the wife of sir Thomas Trevor of Trevallin, in the county of Denbigh, eventually constituted baron of the exchequer, by whom she had no issue. In 1638 lady Trevor received dower amounting to £200 per annum out of the Ireland estate. (*Lanc. and Chesh. Wills*, vol. iii. p. 200.)

Thomas Ireland of Bewsey, esq. (whose funeral certificate has not been found), is described as being sir Thomas's "second son by Margaret Aston his second wife." He gave the information here contained to Randle Holme. He was born about the year 1602, and does not appear to have been distinguished in war or conspicuous in peace, but was probably, like his father, skilled in the law. He was a shrewd man, of some ability, and perhaps of good business habits. He was not slow in vindicating his rights or taking care of his property. It is not to his credit that he sold public lands appropriated to the repair of Warrington bridge without making any other provision for that object (Beamont's *Warrington*, p. 87, note), and in 1635 he had seized or held lands in Burtonwood and Great Sankey, which were claimed by sir Peter Leigh of Lyme, and his unpublished correspondence with Mr. John Bradshaw, a legal agent of sir Peter, on the subject in dispute, does not tend to elevate his character or establish the belief in his fine sense of moral right. Sir Peter Leigh declined to correspond with him, and "resolved not to be troubled in person" by him. Ireland's letters contain some curious passages and striking characteristics of the times, and Bradshaw's rough charge against the lord of Warrington of misrepresentation, exaggeration and duplicity, is yet expressed in courteous phraseology. (*Lanc. MSS.*, vol. xxxviii. pp. 316–17.) Shortly after this misunderstanding with sir Peter Leigh, Edward Sonkey of Sonkey, gent., filed a bill in Chancery against Mr. Ireland for an account of the rents of his estate in Little Sonkey, alleging that being only three years old when his father died, his father's executor, sir Thomas Ireland, entered upon the lands and retained the rents, which Mr. Ireland evidently withheld. The complainant Sonkey stated that from his youth he had been a traveller beyond the seas, and having spent many years abroad, had only recently returned. (Beamont's *Warrington*, note p. 47.) About this time Mr. Ireland was visited with sickness, and died at the early age of 36, leaving issue an only surviving child, Margaret, who is named in this certificate. She married her collateral kinsman sir Gilbert Ireland of Hutte and Hale, knt., who died issueless, at the age of 51, in the year 1675, leaving his widow surviving. Being seized under her father's settlement of his estate, made in 1638, she devised Bewsey and Warrington to her cousin Richard Atherton of Atherton, esq., ancestor of Thomas lord Lilford, the present noble owner. She died in the same year as her husband, aged 45.

The following account of "The order of the funerall of Thomas Irland of Bewsey Esq' from Bewsey to Warrington Church Janii 1638" is from *Harl. MS.* No. 2129, fol. 59.

No poore at all.
First John Gardiner, Tho. Barnes.
Tho. Barton, William Barrow.
Geo. Woods, alone.
Penon of Armes by Piers Gerard.
Helme and Crest by Mr. Tho. Irland.
Cote of Armes by Mr. Jo. Irland of Halwood.
Mr. Bently, Physitian, Mr. Atherton.
Mrs. Barnett, Mr Coe, Mr. Ward, preacher.
The *Corpes* borne by Gents.
Mrs. Margret Irland, hed mourner.
Mrs. Atherton, Mrs. Jeffreyes.
Mrs. Stanley, Mrs. Bankes.
Mrs. Alice Stanley, Mrs Mary Ogles.
Margaret Barlow.
Mr. Jo. Atherton, Mr. Jo. Jeffreyes.
Mr. Bankes, Mr. Tho. Stanley.
Mr. Ja. Bankes, Mr. Geo. Atherton.
Mr. Rich. Allen and his sonne.
Kuts., Gents., &c.

Mr. Ireland's will is dated Bewsey 14th January 1638-9, and was proved at Chester 18th April 1639. At its date he was "sicke in bodye" and died two days afterwards. He desired that his body might be buried "in his Chaple at his parish Church in Warrington soe as it be done in the day and not in the night, with a Sermon by Mr. Ward parson thereof, and with noe more pompe then accordinge to his [testators] degree." (*Lanc. and Chesh. Wills*, vol. iii. p. 199.) There is a touch of parsimony in this testamentary injunction, and the ominous announcement, "no poore at all" at the funeral, which was not solemnized until the 22nd February, is perhaps characteristic of the man. The order of the funeral of this wealthy manerial lord was a deviation at this time from the ordinary mode of conducting funeral pageants in Lancashire. Dr. Whitaker (*Whalley*, p. 505, 3rd ed.) has given an accurate and interesting account of the ruinous expenses which were incurred in the seventeenth century by country gentlemen on the decease of the heads of their houses, and it is just possible that, in this instance, the testator may have provided wisely and well against the prevalent extravagance on these mournful occasions. He may have felt that it was possible to be just and even friendly towards his neighbours without adopting their opinions wholesale, and that moderation and propriety were virtues not to be discarded, whilst reckless and useless expenditure, although fashionable, was to be discountenanced.

The rev. William Ward was presented to the rectory of Warrington by Thomas Ireland, esq. the patron, in the year 1621, and the rev. John Coe (afterwards rector of a mediety of Lymm) was his curate, appointed also by Mr. Ireland. *R.*]

ROBERT EARL OF SUSSEX, 1629.

Funeral Certificate, I. 8. 34 *Coll. Arm.*

THE right honourable Robert Radcliffe Earl of Sussex, Viscount Fitzwalter, Lord Egremont, and Burnell, and Knight of the noble order of the Garter, departed this mortall life at his house in Clerkenwell the xxij[th] daye of September 1629, his body beinge honourably transported from thence, through the Citty of

London, to the Barres without Allgate, was carried to Borham in Essex by Newhall, and buried in y⁰ parrish church there by his noble Auucestors. He maried two wives, Bridget first wife Dā of Sʳ Charles Morison of Caishoberie in the County of Hertford Knight, by whom he had yssue Henry Lo: ffitz-walter, who married Jane Dā and coheire of Sʳ Michaell Stanhop Kᵗ; Thomas Ratcliffe 2ᵈ sonne; Elizabeth first Dā married to Sʳ John Ramsey Knight, Viscount Haddington and Earle of Holdernes; and Honora 2ᵈ daughter; all died without yssue.

He mard to his 2ᵈ wife Francis dā of Hercules Meutas of Hame in the county of Essex Esq. and Pentioner to Queene Elizabeth, by whom he had no yssue. The honor is discended to Sir Edward Ratcliffe Knight, sonne and heire of Sʳ Humphrey Ratcliffe Kᵗ 2ᵈ sonne of Robert Ratcliffe yᵉ first Earle of Sussex, created by K. H. 8. the 8 day of December, in yᵉ 2j yeare of yᵉ said Kings raigne at Whithall. The said right honourable Robt. Earle of Sussex made Mʳ Richard Buckley Executor of his last will and Testament. This Certificate was taken by Samson Lennard Blewmantle officer of Armes.

OSWALD MOSLEY, Esq., 1630.

Original Funeral Certificates of the North in Coll. Arm., No. 6.

OSWALD MOSLEY of Ancotts in the County of Lancaster Esquier departed this mortall life at Ancotts vpon the 9ᵗʰ day of November 1630, and was interred in Manchester church.

He married Anne daughter and coheire to Alexander Lowe of Mile end nere Steppard[33] in the County of Chester gent. by whom he had yssue Nicholas Mosley his sonne and heyre now of the age of 19 yeares or thereabouts at the tyme of his father's death.

[33] Stockport, sometimes written *Stoppart*.

Edward 2 sonne to the defuncte.
Oswald 3 sonne to the defuncte.
Samuell 4 sonne to the defuncte.
Francis 5 sonne to the defuncte.
Anne eldest dau. to the defuncte married Robert Booth of Salford in the county of Lancaster gent. by whom he had yssue Robert, Humphrey and Anne Booth.
Margaret 2 dau. vnmarried.
Mary 3 dau. vnmarried.
This certificate was taken at Ancotts vpon the 26 day of January 1637 by Randle Holme of the Citty of Chester deputy to the office of Armes and testyfied under the hand of Mr Nicholas Mosley sonne and heire to the defuncte.

NICHOLAS MOSLEY.

The pedigree recorded at the Visitation of co. Lanc. anno 1664, commences with Edward Moseley, who by his wife, Margaret, daughter of Alexander Elcock of Hillgate, co. Cest., had issue sir Nicholas Moseley knt., an alderman of London, and Anthony Moseley of Manchester, who married Alice, daughter of Richard Webster of Manchester; by her he had issue the above Oswald, whose wife is stated to have been Anne, daughter and coheir of Raufe Lowe of Mile End, co. Cest. Of their issue mentioned above, the following particulars are stated in the Visitation:

·1. Nicholas, mar^d Jane dau'r of John Lever to Alkrington, co. Lanc., by whom he had Oswald (aged 24 in 1664), Edward, Nicholas, and Anne, Elizth, Jane and Catherine; 2. Edward was of Manchester, and mar^d Meriall, dau'r of Richard Salstonstall of Huntwich, co. York, and had issue, Edward (aged 8), and Anne; 3. Oswald was of Manchester, and appears to have died before 10 Sepember 1664; 4. Samuel was residing in Ireland in 1664; and 5. Francis, of whom nothing more is said in the Visitation; but he was a fellow of the Collegiate church of Manchester. 1. Anne, married Robert Booth of Salford, and afterwards, Thomas Case, a divine; 2. Margaret, married John Angier, a divine; and 3. Mary, married George Crowther, citizen of London. *K.*

[There is a carefully deduced pedigree of Mosley of Ancoats hall in the parish of Manchester in Booker's *Hist. of the Parochial Chapelry of Didsbury*, CHETHAM series, vol. xlii. p. 170; and an etching of the monumental brass in the choir of Manchester cathedral dedicated to the memory of Oswald Mosley of Ancoats, esq., whose funeral certificate is here given, (and who was baptised at the Collegiate church, Manchester, April 26th 1583, and buried there November 11th 1630, æt. 47), in Dr. Hibbert Ware's *Hist. of the Collegiate Church of Manchester*, vol. i. 4to. Also notices of him and his descendants, with an engraving of his monument and a view of Ancoats hall, in sir Oswald Mosley's *Family Memoirs*, pp. 22-25, 4to. 1849, privately printed. *R.*]

EDWARD MOORE, Esq., 1633.

Original Funeral Certificates of the North in Coll. Arm., No. 7.

THE Worlt Edward Moore of Banck Hall in the County of Lancaster Esquire departed this mortall life living within a mile and a halfe of Stone in the County of Stafford and dyed of a Paluesley suddenly in his return from London, and lyth interred in Stone Church in the County aforesayd. He dyed vpon the 28 November 1633.

The sayd defuncte married Katherine daughter of John Hocknoll of Prenton in the County of Chester Esquier by whom she had yssue John More now of Bank Hall aforsayd Esquire sonne and heyre, at the takinge of this certyficate is 38 yeares ould or therabout and at his fathers death about 33 yeares ould. W[cb] sayd John Moore married Mary daughter of Alexander Rigby of Bourgh in the County of Lan[c] Esq[r] by whom she had yssue Edward, Alexander and Katherine Moore.

Robert Moore second sonne to the defuncte now vnmarried 1638. Thomas 3 sonne to the defuncte dyed since his father's death without yssue. Elinor eldest daughter to the defuncte married William Ireland of Leuerpoole in the County of Lancaster by whom she hath noe yssue.

Elizabeth second daughter to the defuncte married James Bailey a Scotchman now of Irland by whom she hath noe yssue.

Victoria yongest daughter to the defuncte not yet married.

This Certyficate was taken at Leuerpoole aforsayd upon the 23th day of Aprill 1638, beinge 4 yeares or more after the death of the sayd Edward Moore Esq[r] and was taken by Randle Holme of the Citty of Chester, gentleman, deputy of the office of Armes, and certyfied under the hand of M[rs] Katherine Moore late wife and Administratrix to the defuncte.

KATHEREN MOORE.

At the Visitation of the co. of Lancaster a[o] 1567, a pedigree of Moore of Bank hall was registered, commencing with Thomas More of Liverpool, who married Cicely, daughter and sole heir of Nicholas Turton of Eccleshall, co. Lancaster, from whom in the seventh generation descended William Moore of Bank hall, esq., who married Jane, daughter of James Lightoulers, and had issue John his eldest son. The arms are tricked in pencil only by the Herald. There is no pedigree of these Moores in the subsequent Visitations. K.

[Edward Moore the head of a family which had uninterruptedly possessed Bank hall, near Liverpool, from the earliest part of the thirteenth century, married about the year 1595 Katherine, daughter of John Hockenhall of Prenton in Wirrall, esq. In 1621 Edward Moore was sheriff of Lancashire. In 1625 he represented Liverpool in parliament, along with James, lord Strange, but did not retain his honour, under the Stanley influence in the borough, in the next parliament. He held strong protestant opinions, and made his Roman catholic neighbours writhe under the oppressive power of the Star chamber of which he was a ready agent. In 1631 sir William Norris of Speak, a dashing soldier and a recusant, censured Moore's harsh conduct as a magistrate in enforcing the penal laws, and opprobrious language was unceremoniously interchanged between these neighbours. Moore "feared not to touche the best," and gave the soldier "the lie;" Norris drew his sword and struck Moore twice. For thus assaulting a justice of the peace he was fined 1000*l.*, committed to prison, and made to pay 50*l.* to Moore. After a turbulent life, Edward Moore died of a sudden attack of pleurisy, whilst on a journey from London to Liverpool in the winter of 1633. He was succeeded by his eldest son John Moore mentioned in this certificate, born about the year 1600, a deputy lieutenant and magistrate of the county of Lancaster. He married in 1633 Mary, daughter of Alexander Rigby of Burgh, esq. In 1640 he was burgess in parliament for Liverpool, and joining the republican party, became one of the Lancashire sequestrators, ranger of Knowsley park, and one of the most active tools of the popular party. He was appointed governor of Liverpool, and became a colonel for the parliament. He sat on the king's trial, and signed his death warrant. Being with his regiment in Ireland, and the plague, flux, and fever every where raging, he died in June 1650 " of a pleurisie, some say of a feaver." It is somewhat remarkable that the father and son died of the same disorder. Edward Moore, the son and successor of the regicide, was created a baronet in 1675, which title expired with sir William Moore the fifth baronet in the year 1810. The *Rental* of sir Edward Moore, the careful but vindictive son of an unfortunate and disaffected father, has been printed by the Chetham society (vol. xii.), with an excellent Introduction, and some valuable notes by the editor, Thomas Heywood, esq. This funeral certificate supplies several genealogical facts which had escaped the research of Mr. Heywood. *R.*]

RICHARD BOLD, Esq., 1635.

Funeral Certificates, I. 24. 52ᵇ *Coll. Arm.*

RICHARD Bould of Bould, in the county of Lancaster, Esquier, Departed this mortall life at Bould aforesaid, upon the xix^th day of February 1635, and was interred in Farnworth church, in the said county. He married Anne dā to Sir Peter Leigh of Lime in the county of Chester knight, by whom he had yssue Richard Bould his eldest sonne, which dyed in his fathers lifetyme. Peter Bould now sonne and heire of the age of ix yeares or there about at yᵉ tyme of his fathers decease. Margarett eldest Dā: to the defunct. Mary 2ⁿᵈ Dā: Katherin 3ᵈ Dā: Anne 4ᵗʰ Dā: Frances 5ᵗʰ Dā: Radcliffe 6ᵗʰ Dā: to yᵉ defunct, all unmarried. This Certificate was taken at Bould upon the 4th Dā: of March 1635 by Randle Holme of the Citty of Chester, Deputie to the office of Armes, and testified under the hand of Anne late wife and sole Executrix to the defunct.

ANNE BOULD.

The pedigree of this ancient family was registered at the Visitation Aᵒ 1664, deducing the descent from Ricardus de Bolde, in co. Lanc., in the reign of king Stephen. Peter Bold, eldest surviving son, and heir of the defunct, married Joane, daughter of sir Ralphe Assheton of Whalley, in co. Lanc., bart., and died in 1658; by her he had issue, Richard, who *ob. juv.*, and Peter Bold aged 8 years in 1664; Margaret, eldest daughter of the defunct, became the wife of Edward Morgill of Chester; Mary, the second daughter, married John Atherton of Atherton, co. Lanc., esq.; Catherine, the third daughter, married Roger Pritchard of Wales; Anne, the fourth daughter, died unmarried; Frances, the fifth daughter, married Henry Ogle of Whiston, co. Lanc.; and Ratcliffe, the youngest daughter, married James Dukenfield of Hindley, co. Lanc. Arms *argent a griffin segreant sable*.

[See Baines's *Hist. of Lanc.* vol. iii. p. 717, where the pedigree of the family is given; also a view of Bold hall, and an etching of the monument erected in the Bold chapel within Farnworth church, to the memory of Richard Bold of Bold, esq., the defunct, who died on the 19th February 1635, aged 47 years. For an account of the family chapel see canon Raines's *Hist. of Lanc. Chantries*, CHETHAM series, vol. i. p. 76; and for notices of the Bolds, *Gent. Mag.*, vol. xciv. pt. ii. p. 198; Gregson's *Fragments of Lanc.*; *Lanc. MSS.*, vol. xii.; and *Stanley Papers*, pt. ii. p. 113, note, CHETHAM series. *R.*]

RICHARD VISCOUNT MOLYNEUX, 1636.

Funeral Certificate in the Public Record Office.

THE right ho^ble Sr Richard Molineux of Sefton in the county of Lancaster Knt. the second Baronet (created 22nd May in the 9th yeare of King James) and after made Viscount Molineux of Mariburgh in the kingdom of Ireland by our Sovereign Lord King Charles in the .... yeare of his raigne, departed this mortall life at Sefton aforesaid 8th of May 1636, where he lyeth interred. He married Mary, daughter and one of the coheires of Sir Thomas Carrell of Sussex Knt. by whom he had issue Richard Molineux, eldest sonne, now Viscount Molineux of Mariburgh, who married Mary, daughter to James Lord Strange, heire apparent to William Earle of Derby, Lord Stanley, Strange of Knocking and of the Isle of Man, and Knight of the Most Noble Order of the Garter; Carrell second sonne.

In 1779 a pedigree was recorded of this family, commencing with sir Richard Molineux of Sefton, who was knighted at the coronation of queen Mary. He died in 1567, having married Eleanor, daughter of sir Alexander Radcliffe of Ordsall, co. Lanc., knt., and by whom he had issue, William Molineux his eldest son, who died in the lifetime of his father in the same year. He married Bridget, the daughter of John Lascelles, esq^re, attorney-general of the duchy of Lancaster, by whom he had issue, sir Richard Molineux, knt., knighted by queen Elizabeth 24th June 1586, then aged 26, and was the secondly created baronet on the first creation of that order by king James, being advanced to the dignity on the 22nd May, 9 Jac. He married Frances, daughter of sir Gilbert Gerard, knt., master of the rolls, by whom he had issue, sir Richard Molineux *the Defunct*, subject of the above certificate, who was created viscount Molineux of Maryborough, in the peerage of Ireland, by patent, 22nd December 1628. He married Mary, daughter and coheir of sir Thomas Caryll of Benton, co. Sussex, knt., by whom he had issue, 1. Richard Molineux, second viscount Molineux, his eldest son, who married Frances, daughter of William Seymour, marquis of Hertford, and afterwards duke of Somerset, but died about 1651 without issue; 2. Caryll Molineux, who succeeded his brother as viscount Molineux (ancestor of the present earl of Sefton), and who married Mary, daughter of sir Alexander Barlow of Barlow, co. Lanc., knt., and died 2nd February 1698-9; and two daughters, 1. Elizabeth, wife of sir William Stanley of Hooton, co. Chester, baronet; 2. Mary, wife of sir George Selby of Whitehouse, in the bishopric of Durham, baronet. (This is the only issue given in the pedigree of 1779.)

The pedigree of Molineux is deduced from William des Molins, first lord of Sefton, by grant of Roger de Poictiers, from a grant of William the Conqueror, and a copy of the descent, with the arms to each match, is amongst Vincent's *MSS.* in this college (No. 23, p. 30). *K.*

[He succeeded his father in 16—, and was contracted in marriage during his minority to Fleetwood, daughter and heiress of Richard Barton of Barton, esq., but from whom he was divorced by sentence of the consistory court of Chester, 15th February 1607, and she afterwards became the wife, first, of Richard Shuttleworth of Gawthorp, esq.; and secondly, of Thomas Stanley of Eccleston, esq. (*Lanc. MSS.* vol. xii.)

Sir Richard Molineux married Mary, daughter and coheir of sir Thomas Caryll of Benton, co. Sussex, knt., by whom he had issue, 1. Richard, betrothed in his early years, but not married, to Henriette Marie, daughter of James the 7th earl of Derby, K.G.; he afterwards married lady Frances Seymour, daughter of the duke of Somerset, and the descendant maternally of Charles duke of Suffolk, by Mary, queen dowager of France, daughter of king Henry VII., but ob. s.p.; 2. Caryll; 3. Philip; 4. Frances; 5. Elizabeth; and 6. Mary.

He was created viscount Molyneux of Maryburgh in Ireland on the 22nd December 4 Car. 1628, and died in the year 1636 (and not 1632 as stated in the peerages, and also in the family pedigree in Baines's *Hist. of Lanc.*, vol. iv. p. 216). His relict died "at her house in St. Martin's Lane in the Fields, London" in 1639. *R.*]

ALICE, COUNTESS OF DERBY, 1636-7.

Funeral Certificate, I. 8.   53^h Coll. Arms.

THE right honourable Lady Alice Countesse Dowager of Derby departed this mortall life at her house at Harust in the county of Middlesex the 23^d day of January 1636. She was first the wife of Ferdynando Lord Stanley Strang and of the Isle of Man, the fifth Earl of Derby ; she was dā. of Sir John Spencer Knight and aunt of Robert the first Baron Spencer of Wormleighton in the county of North'ton. She was 2dly maried to Sir Thomas Egerton Knight Lord Elsmere Viscount Brackley and Lord Chauncellor of England, by whom she had no yssue. But by her first husband she had yssue 3 daughters his heires generall. Anne the eldest mar^d to Gray Bridges Lord Chandos of Shudeley Castle in Gloucestershire. Frances the 2^d maried to Sir John Egerton Kn^t now Earl of Bridgwater 2^d sonne and heire mayle of the foresaid Sir Thomas Egerton Lord Chauncellor aforesaid. Elizabeth ye youngest maried to Henry Lord Hastings now Earl of Huntington. She left her sole Executor the right honourable Henry Montague Earle of Manchester Viscount Mandeuile and Lord Kymbolton Lord Priuy Seale who hath attested the truth of this Certificate which was taken by William Riley Blewmantle Officer of Armes.

MANCHESTER.

[Alice, the eleventh and youngest child of sir John Spencer of Wormleighton in the county of Warwick, and of Althorp in the county of Northants, knt., M.P., and of his wife, Katharine, daughter of sir Thomas Kitson of Hengrave in the county of Suffolk, knt., was born about the year 1556. Her five older sisters were married to men of high rank and great wealth, and all her brothers seem to have been distinguished by their social position and, like their father, for their bountiful house-keeping and almost princely munificence. Robert, first lord Spencer (so created July 21st 1603), was grandson of sir John and nephew of

Alice, lady Derby, and when king James ascended the English throne
was represented to be the richest monied man in the kingdom. Ferdinando, lord Strange, was born about the year 1558, and married
Alice, daughter of sir John Spencer, in 1579. She appears to have
been a great favourite with her husband's father, earl Henry, as she,
her husband and their children were constantly at Knowsley and Lathom house. (Vide *Stanley Papers*, pt. ii.) It is evident from a letter
addressed by queen Elizabeth to Henry lord Strange December 6th
1571, that more than one eldest son of the house of Stanley has been
regarded as an honourable hostage, and kept in gentle durance by the
sovereign, and that the fourth as well as the first earl might have said:
"My son .... Stanley is frank'd up in hold," (*Ric. III.*, act iv. sc. v.)
although the opposition of earl Henry, if at any time adverse to the
queen, would be faint and timid. Her majesty writes: "By your letters
Dear Coosyn your wiffe and otherwise also we understand how well and
ernestly disposed you are towards us and our service, and that the
cause of your absence from hence is not other than to attend uppon our
Coosyn your Father now in his sicknes and thereby also in tyme of his
sicknes to have regard for the good order of this country, for the continuance of the same quietnes, all which we do very well allow in you,
and in such respect we are the better content with your long absence:
and knowing your ernest goodwill to serve and please us at all tymes
the lyke wherof we are sorry not to have found in your Brother which
we know cannot but be displeasant to our Coosyn your good Father
whom we have great cause to love and esteem for his approved fidelitie
to us in these tymes. . . . . . We will not otherwise therefore at this
tyme direct you to repayre hyther than yourselfe shall see may stand
with your father's lyking in his sycknes, but yet considering your absence we have been ernest with our Coosyn your wife that she wold
move you to send up youre Eldest Sone to be here some tyme that
both we might see hym and his Mother might have some comfort of
him, and chiefly that he might here learn some nurture and be fashioned
in good manners mete for one such as he is and hereafter shall be by
cours of nature mete to serve the Realm. And so we conclude with
this ernest request and our commendations to your Father, to whom we
hartely wish amendment in Helth: and with his good lyking you may
send hym up to be here this Christmas and which we will now assuredly

look for." (Murdin's *State Pap.*, p. 185.) The jealousy of the queen could only be allayed by the presence of the youthful Ferdinando at court, who naturally enough at this time lingered about the sick chamber of his venerable grandfather. Like her royal predecessor, Elizabeth had hard thoughts of the Stanleys, and her suspicions were excited by the absence of three generations from her immediate presence — " Cold friends to me: what do they in the North, when they should serve their Sovereign?" (*Ric. III.*, act iv. sc. iv.) And so doubtless the caprice if not cruelty of the queen was gratified, and the young stripling, now in his fourteenth year, was sent to Windsor. Lord Strange does not appear to have filled any office about the court, although so nearly allied to the queen, his grandmother being her majesty's first cousin and granddaughter of Henry VII., and he was connected in other ways with most of the noblest families in the kingdom. Lord Strange and his wife were however received with marks of high confidence and favour by the queen, and the former, as a young man, was present in the year 1575, when Elizabeth was at Worcester on her way to Woodstock, acccompanied by five bishops, a large number of the nobility, and many ladies of the highest rank, and when all that chivalry and romance could evolve of pomp, pride and circumstance, was in requisition to honour the queen and grace her progress. (Nichols's *Prog. of Queen Eliz.*, vol. i.)

On January 1st 1574-5, a new year's gift was presented to the queen by the youthful lord Strange, viz., "an eare picke of gold enamuled, garnished with sparcks of rubyes, blue saphires and seede pearle, dim. oz. dim.9⁴." And on the 1st January 1575-6, lord Strange again presented to her Majesty "a jewell of golde, beinge a Squyrrell sett with iii sparcks of dyamondes, iii sparcks of emeraldes, and iv sparcks of rubyes, with iii mene perles." (*Ibid.*) Lord and lady Strange do not appear to have been always present at the delivery of the sermons of the great Lancashire puritan preachers at Lathom and Knowsley, in the time of earl Henry, but in 1577 lord Strange was one of the auditors of "A Sermon Preached before the Right Hon. the Earle of Darbie, and divers others, assembled in His Honor's Chappel at Newparke, in Lancashire, the 2nd Januarie 1577, by John Caldwell, Parson of Winwick. Black letter 4to. Dedicated to the Earl. Printed by Thomas East, London, 13th March 1577."[34]

[34] There is a copy of this very scarce sermon in the library at Knowsley.

LANCASHIRE FUNERAL CERTIFICATES. 65

Lord Strange, from the earliest period, was interested in the court revels, theatricals and masques, which would introduce to his notice the poets and artists of the period. "A Historie of Love and Fortune was shewed before Her Majestie at Windsor on the Sondaie at night next before New Years daie 1582, enacted by the Earle of Derbie's Servantes:" And "Sundry Featcs of Tumbling and Activitie were showed before Her Matie on New Years Daie at night by the Lord Straunge his Servants; for which was bought and imploied xxi yards of cotton for the matachins, iii ells of sarcenet and viii pair of gloves." (Cunningham's *Accounts of the Court Revels*, p. 177.) Lord Strange is said to have "distempered his health by vehement exercise," and we know that he entered into the fashionable recreations of stag hunting, hawking and coursing with his neighbours in Lancashire (*Stanley Papers*, pt. ii. pp. 45, 57, 76), and probably practised tilting in the south, as his portrait, now at Worden, was painted with the helmet and tilting spear as adjuncts to the picture. (*Ibid.* p. lxiii.)

On Wednesday January 6th 1587–8, lord Strange's youngest daughter, Elizabeth (apparently named after the queen), was christened at Knowsley, on which occasion the high sheriff, a great party, "and many gentlewomen, came to the christening" banquet. (*Ibid.* p. 46.) It was not until Wednesday the 3rd of February, nearly a month afterwards, that the bishop of Chester arrived at Knowsley, and lady Strange was "churched" in the presence of a great assembly of relatives and friends, lord Strange being absent at Stoneleigh Abbey with his brother-in-law, Mr. Leigh (who married lady Strange's sister), and did not return to Knowsley until the following Saturday, when he found the bishop and many guests awaiting his arrival. (*Ibid.* p. 48.) On Friday 27th September 1588, "Lady Strange and the little children of hers" came to New park, the earl having arrived on the preceding day, (*ibid.* p. 50,) but it was not until Saturday the 2nd November, that "my Lord Straunge retorned from London," (*ibid.* p. 52,) and on the Wednesday following he and lord Dudley again went to London, lady Strange in the mean time remaining with the earl, and lord Strange "not coming home" to Lathom house from London until Tuesday 4th January 1588–9. (*Ibid.* p. 57.) This long absence in London had doubtless some connection with the public alarm on the subject of the Spanish invasion, lord Strange being mayor of Liverpool in 1588, and having

K

taken a prominent part in organizing the defences of the county, and also having raised a large force of horsemen for that purpose.

On Tuesday the 25th January 1588-9, the earl and lord and lady Strange left Lathom house for London, the children of the latter having been sent away under the charge of Edward Stanley, esq. (their father's bachelor uncle), on the preceding day. (*Ibid.* p. 58.)

On Wednesday July 15th 1589, lord Strange and his three daughters arrived at Knowsley, from a visit to sir John Byron (*ibid.* p. 62,) either at Clayton hall or Newstead. September 17th 1589, "Ferdinando lord Stanley and Strange," sir John Spencer (his brother-in-law), and sir George Carew (afterwards earl of Totnes), were created masters of arts at Oxford (Wood's *Fasti* [Bliss], vol. i. p. 250), sir Christopher Hatton having just been appointed chancellor of the University. In March 1589-90, we again find lord and lady Strange at Knowsley, exceedingly popular, surrounded by all the old families of the county, whom they daily received at their hospitable mansions, and in return visited their country friends in the most social manner, dining at Holker, Rufford, Cross hall, Croxteth, and other houses during their sojourn in Lancashire. (*Stanley Papers*, pt. ii.) He attended the spring assize at Lancaster in April 1590, "concerning Mr. Baron of Walton's (Newton's) cawses," which required the advocacy of powerful relatives and friends, and remained there, doubtless watching the curious proceedings with more than ordinary interest, all the week. (*Ibid.* p. 78, and p. 97, note.) Shortly afterwards he and his wife went to London, "the children staying behind" and their father returning again to Knowsley in August of that year. (*Ibid.* pp. 79, 90.)

Ferdinando lord Strange succeeded his father as fifth earl of Derby on the 25th September 1593. On the 12th October following appeared "A Ballad by John Dauter, entitled, Lancashire's Lamentation for the death of the Noble Erle of Derbie" (*Notes and Queries*, 3rd series, vol. i. p. 401), and other poets also bewailed the nation's loss. At Christmas 1593, the young earl was elected a governor of the free grammar school of queen Elizabeth, in Blackburn, and contributed "of benevolence money" to the *Domus* fund xx^s, and his friend "Thomas Gerard of Bryn, gent.," was also elected, and made a similar contribution, at the same time; (*Lanc. MSS., Blackburn School.*) Mr. Yates, a learned Greek scholar being the head master, and two of his pupils being Robert Bolton and "golden-mouthed" Anderton; the first afterwards becoming a distinguished English churchman, of the Puritan type, and the latter a Roman catholic (see *Life of Bolton*, vol. i. pp. 9, 14, 4to, 1641), and both of them Lancashire men. The young nobleman survived his popular father little more than six months, and died, according to the credulity of the age, of witchcraft or poison, after a short illness, at Lathom house, on the 16th April 1594, at the age of 35 years. According to the suspicious rumours and exaggerations of the time, dangerous and insidious proposals were supposed to have been made to him by the Roman catholic party, in connection with the succession to the crown on the anticipated death of Elizabeth, which his integrity and loyalty led him immediately to reject, and it was currently reported, and believed by many, that the disappointed party had effected his death by poison. It is fortunate that a minute contemporaneous account of his disorder and its symptoms has been preserved, and there is no need, from the evidence in that record, to attribute his death either to the effects of witchcraft or poison. "One excellent speech among many," we are told, "cannot be omitted, in the time of his sickness, especially on the day before he departed, at which time he desired one of his doctors, whom he especially loved, to persuade him no longer to live; because," said he, "although out of thy love thou wouldest stir up hopes of life, and dost employ all thy wit, art, and travail to that end; yet knowing for a certainty that I must now die, I pray thee cease, for I am resolved presently to die, and to take away with me only one part of my arms, I mean the Eagle's Wings, so will I fly swiftly into the bosom of CHRIST, my only Saviour; and with that he sent for his lady, and gave her his last farewell, desiring her to take away and love his Doctor, and also to give him some jewel, with his arms and name that he might be remembered, which thing immediately after his death was most honourably performed." His spiritual physicians were Chaderton, bishop of Chester, and Mr. William Leigh, B.D., the learned rector of Standish, who was the earl's domestic chaplain, and had, in early life, been his tutor (*Stanley Papers*, pt. ii. p. 117, note), having filled both the offices of tutor and chaplain to prince Henry, son of James I. (*Royal Household Books* pub. by Soc. of Antiq. p. 329, 4to, 1790.) The physicians who attended the earl were Dr. Canon, Dr. Joyner, Dr. Bate, and Dr. Case — one of their number, at least, living in Chester. (*Harl. MS.*,

247, fo. 204-5; *Gent. Mag.*, vol. xxi. p. 269.) Notwithstanding his dangerous proximity to the crown, lord Strange had always been regarded as a loyal subject to the queen, although without influence at court, and if not employed officially in the service of his country, his patriotism was never questioned. He appears to have been considered by his contemporaries a man of liberal acquirements, and it is certain that his popularity was equal to his abilities and accomplishments. He had a taste for the fashionable and romantic amusements of the day, and was the patron and associate of men of letters. He also had the reputation of being himself a poet. It was of him, under the name of AMYNTAS, that Edmund Spenser sang in "Colin Clout:"

> He, whilst he liv'd, was the noblest swain
> That ever piped on an oaten quill;
> Both did he other, which could pipe, maintain,
> And eke, could pipe himself with passing skill. (p. 34.)

It is to be regretted that the productions of lord Strange are unknown, although some of his occasional pieces without his name were published in 1610, in a collection of English poems, entitled "Belvedere, or the Garden of the Muses," with those of the more celebrated poets of his time. It is not to be supposed that a poet like Spenser, to whom he was personally known, and who claimed relationship to lady Strange, would have described him adventitiously as a poet, had he not merited the distinction.

There are two portraits of this earl, one of them at Knowsley and the other at Newhall, the seat of sir Robert T. Gerard, bart., and the features in both bear a striking resemblance to the portrait at Worden hall, of which there is an etching in the *Stanley Papers*, pt. ii. p. lxiii. The build is light, the complexion fair, the hair dark-brown, the beard peaked, and, like the moustache, sandy. The eyes are blue, and the artist has not omitted the wart on the forehead. The expression is singularly amiable and intelligent. The portrait at Knowsley is a bust, and he wears a black velvet doublet, and an open lace-edged collar. In the large picture at Newhall there are two figures, half length. The earl is pourtrayed arm in arm with his friend and neighbour Mr. (afterwards sir Thomas) Gerard of Brynn. Both are dressed in black velvet doublets and open lace collars, lord Strange's hand resting on his sword, and Mr. Gerard's on a skull. Their arms and titles are on the background. There is no date, but as the earl does not appear to be more than about 26 or 28, and his singularly handsome-looking friend some years older, the portraits would be taken whilst he was lord Strange. The artist is unknown.

The earl left issue the three daughters and coheiresses mentioned in this funeral certificate, their father being the heir general of Joan, wife of sir George Stanley, and sole daughter and heiress of John lord Strange and Mohun, son and heir of Richard, lord Strange of Knockyn, grandson of John, lord Mohun of Dunster, one of the founders of the most noble order of the Garter. (Beltz's *Memor. of the Order of the Garter*, p. 51.) The eldest daughter, the lady Anne, was born May 1580, the lady Frances August 1583, and the lady Elizabeth January 1587-8.

Shortly after the death of her husband lady Derby commenced the famous law suits with William the sixth earl of Derby, respecting his title to the Isle of Man and other hereditary estates of the Stanley family. On the 23rd September 1594, Mr. Michael Doughtie, servant of William earl of Derby, and Mr. Hugh Ellis, servant to the lady Alice countess dowager of Derby, deposited in the presence of Francis lord Bacon and others, a trunk containing family evidences, in the custody of sir Thomas Egerton, afterwards lord Ellesmere. (*Egerton Papers*, p. 205, CAMDEN Soc.) Her ladyship was still in favour at court, and apparently well acquainted with the queen's tastes and foibles, as on the 1st of January 1599-1600, "the countes of Darby, wydow" of earl Ferdinando, presented to her majesty "one pettycote without bodyes [bodice] of silver tynsell, wrought in squares, with a border of trees of grene sylke needlework;" and the queen's new year's gift to "the countess of Darby, wydow," was a piece of " guilt Plate, K. 21 oz. di. di. 9^r. (Nichols's *Prog. Queen Eliz.*, vol. i.)

The profound legal and judicial ability of sir Thomas Egerton, afterwards the lord chancellor, secured for the dowager countess of Derby and her daughters a larger portion of the old hereditary estates and titles of the Stanleys than any of the parties interested in them had originally anticipated. In the year 1599 he had the misfortune to lose both his eldest son sir Thomas Egerton, a young man of great promise, and also his second wife. Under the double affliction, it was said that "the Lord Keeper doth sorrow more than the wisdom of soe great a man ought to doe. He keepes privat, hath desired Judge Gawdy to sit in Chancery, and yt is thought that he will not come abroade this tearme." (Sydney *State Papers*, p. 301.) However, in the year 1600, a few months afterwards, at the mature age of sixty, the handsome lord keeper Egerton married, for his third wife, the accomplished dowager lady Derby, who at that time was noted for her vivacity and great personal charms; although she was no longer the youthful *Amaryllis* of Spenser, having attained the age of 44 years. The genial old chancellor did not think with his great contemporary and saturnine friend, Francis lord Bacon, that it was "impossible to love and be wise," (*Essay on Love,*) but as the queen's sanction had not been secured, the wisdom of the step was, at least, questionable. "Upon Tuesday morning (says Sir Rowland Whyte, writing to Sir Robert Sydney Oct. 24, 1600), my Lord Keeper married the Countess Dowager of Darby, which is made knowen to the Queen, but how she takes it I doe not heare. Yt is given out that his sonne, Mr. John Egerton shall marrie her second daughter, and that the young Lord Hastings shall marry her third daughter." Both these matches took place. Sir John Harrington of Exton wrote an ode or epigram "In prayse of the Countess of Darby, married to the Lord Chancellor," (6. 14. *Epigr.* 47), and complimented the matronly bride by saying: "She lived—ah! too, too long in widow's state."

> This noble countess lived many yeares
> With Derby, one of England's greatest peeres;
> Fruitful and faire, and of so cleare a name
> That all this region marvell'd at her fame.
> But this brave peere extinct by hasten'd fate,
> She lived, ah! too, too long in widow's state;
> And in that state, took such sweet state upon her,
> All cares, eyes, tongues, heard, saw, and spoke, her honour.

In the year after her marriage (1601), sir Edmund Anderson, the chief justice, conveyed by sale Harefield place in Middlesex, three miles from Uxbridge, "to Sir Thomas Egerton, Lord Keeper, to his wife Alice, Countess Dowager of Derby, and to the Ladies Ann, Frances and Elizabeth Stanley her daughters" (Lysons' *Parishes of Middlesex*, pp. 122-3), from which it appears that this delightful place had been purchased by the Stanleys. It was settled upon the countess for her life, with the reversion to the eldest son of her eldest daughter, who ultimately succeeded to the estate. Lord Campbell states, on insufficient authority, that Harefield was the property of lord Ellesmere, whose residence here, however, only commenced at the time of his third marriage. It was in the autumn of 1602 that queen Elizabeth paid a three days' visit to those distinguished personages, and here Shakespeare's immortal *Othello* was performed for the first time before the queen, and here Ben Jonson is said to have contributed to her majesty's amusement by the production of a masque, or at least a lottery, with quaint poetical and allegorical devices. (Lodge's *Illustr.*, vol. iii. p. 132; Nichols's *Prog. Queen Eliz.*, vol. ii. pp. 20, 21; Campbell's *Lives of the Chancellors*, vol. ii. p. 207.)

In 1603 the dowager lady Derby rode on horseback on king James' triumphant entry into London to take possession of the English crown. (Nichols's *Prog. James I.* p. 174.) In August 1607 on visiting her youngest daughter Elizabeth, countess of Huntingdon at Castle Ashby, a masque, written by Marston, was performed in honour of the lady-mother, and was afterwards published and dedicated to the countess dowager of Derby. (*Ibid.* p. 43.) In 1609 John Davis of Hereford addressed a metrical dedication to the "well accomplished Lady Alice Countess of Derby, and her three right noble daughters, by birth nature and education," of his poem called "The Holy Roode, or Christ's Crosse, containing Christ Crucified, described in speaking picture." 4to, pp. 80. The same writer in his *Microcosmos*, 4to, 1603, pp. 300, celebrates in his preface, amongst other distinguished characters,

———— Egerton famouzed
For love to equity; chief justice of the land;

and Edward Bulkley, D.D., rector of Odell in Bedfordshire, dedicated his *Apologie for Religion*, 4to, pp. 176, 1602, "to the right hon. sir Thomas Egerton, knt., lord keeper, chamberlain of the county palatine of Chester," and therein states "that as his book was written for the good of God's Church, so he had been encouraged to offer and present it to the Lord Keeper as a true testimony of a loving heart, and of dutiful affection towards his honour." Robert Hill, B.D., lecturer of St. Martin's-in-the-Fields, and rector of St. Margaret's, Friday street, London, in his *Pathway to Prayer and Piety*, 12mo, 1609, pp. 432, 3rd ed., dedicated to Thomas lord chancellor Ellesmere, describes his patron, in a well written "Epistle Dedicatorie," as "a trustie counsellour to our gracious King, an vpright Judge to our Christian people, and a good Patron to the despised Clergie," subscribing himselfe "from your Parish of St. Martin-in-the-Fields November 17th 1608." Lord Ellesmere was honourably distinguished for his support of the English church and clergy, and seems to have had more books dedicated to him than any of his contemporaries. In disposing of his patronage, one of the clergy stated "Your Honour will not give to that Jacob bleare-eyed Leah, who hath served many a year for fair Rachel. You will not make him a Shepheard of men's soules who is rather fit to be a shepheard of men's sheepe. What good you have done to this Church of ours let Churchmen judge. You love our nation. You have rebuilt for us many decaied Synagogues, and put many poore Preachers into the pool of Bethesda, who have bin thus cured of their long disease of Povertie without the descending of any one Angel." On 15th March 1617 full of years and honour the lord chancellor expired in London, and was buried at Doddlestone in Cheshire, his widow continuing to live after his death at Harefield place; and it was here, that about the year 1635 Milton's beautiful pastoral, *Arcades*, was written in compliment, and presented to the same countess dowager, in her second widowhood, by some of her grandchildren. In this scenic representation the great poet, who resided at that time with his father at Horton adjacent to Harefield, complimented the lord chancellor's widow in these glowing strains:

> Here you shall have greater grace
> To serve the Lady of this place;
> Such a rural Queen
> All Arcadia hath not seen.

Milton's connection with this cultivated and intellectual family also led to the composition of the delightful masque of *Comus*.

The countess dowager of Derby, like both her husbands, was the patron of some of the most celebrated writers and poets of the Elizabethan and Jacobean period, as Mr. Heywood has shewn in his interesting volume on the subject, to which, it will be seen, an addition of several names may be made.

The countess died at Harefield place on the 23rd and was buried on the 28th January 1636-7, aged about 81 years, and was buried in the church of the B. V. Mary, having survived her first husband nearly 43 years. Her monument is engraved by Lysons. Her son-in-law lord Chandos succeeded her at Harefield, pursuant to the deed of purchase in 1601. Her portrait at Knowsley on panel represents her as a very handsome woman with chestnut-coloured hair, small black head dress, large Elizabethan ruff, sleeves and stomacher, covered with lace. She holds a feather fan in her left hand. On the canvas is painted "Anno 1598 æt. suæ 42." This fine picture has never been engraved, although Lysons refers to a very rare engraved portrait of this countess, without the engraver's name. It may be added, that the quarterings borne by Ferdinando earl of Derby on his shield, and allowed by the heralds in 1594, were as follows: 1. Stanley; 2. Latham; 3. Man; 4. Warren; 5. Strange; 6. Woodvile; 7. Mohun; 8. Montalt; 9. Brandon; 10. Bruin; 11. Rokeby; 12. Stanley. *R.*]

GEORGE CLARKE, 1637.

Original Funeral Certificates of the North in Coll. Arms.

MR. George Clarke of Manchester in the County of Lancaster Haberdasher departed this mortall life at his house in Manchester aforsayd upon the —— day of October 1637, and was interred in Manchester church.

The sayd defunctem married —— daughter to Edmund Gee of Manchester aforsayd by whom he had no yssue, leaving his estate vnto diuers pious vses.

This certificate was taken at Manchester upon the 28 day of January 1637[-8] by Randle Holme of the City of Chester deputy to the office of Armes and testified vnder the hand . . . . . .

There is no pedigree of George Clarke in the Visitations of Lancashire, nor of the family of Gee with whom he intermarried. In the margin of his funeral certificate it is stated "noe Armes prod." Fuller, in his *Worthies*, mentions him as being an "Haberdasher, a plain, honest man, just, temperate, and frugal; and according to his understanding (which in the world's esteem was not great) devout, a daily frequenter of the Prayers in the Colledge Church, and the hearer of Sermons there. Not long before the breaking forth of our Civil dissensions, dying without issue, he made the poor his heir, and did give them one hundred pounds per annum, in good lands lying in a place called Crompsall, within a mile of Manchester. I have not yet obtained the certain date of his death." (Vol. ii. p. 214, ed. Dr. Nuttall, 1840.) The benefaction is recorded in the *Report of the Commissioners on Charities*, vol. xvi. p. 138. K.

[On the 13th December, 1636, Mr. Clarke settled by indenture of feoffment of this date, made between himself (described as George Clarke of Manchester, haberdasher) of the one part, and Humphrey Chetham of Clayton, esq., Nicholas Mosley of Ancoates, esq., Richard Radcliffe, gent. (son and heir-apparent of William Radcliffe of Manchester, esq.), Samuel Tippinge of Manchester, gent., Francis Mosley of the same, gent., Henry Johnson the elder, mercer, John Hartley, draper, John Gaskell, draper, William Radley, gent., Ralph Worsley of Platt-within-Rusholme, gent., John Marler, gent., Richard Lomax, clothier, Thomas Keley, chapman, and John Griffin, chapman (all of Manchester), of the other part, whereby certain messuages and lands in Manchester, Crumpsall, and Totlow, in the county of Lancaster, (subject to two yearly chief rents of 20s. and 2s., so settled by Walter Nugent and Margaret his mother, for the use of the poor, in 1609,) were conveyed to the trustees to hold for the use of the said George Clarke during his natural life, and from and immediately after his death then to hold for the use as to one full moiety to Alice, then wife of the said George Clarke, for her life in satisfaction of dower, and from and after the death of the said Alice, to hold the whole of the messuages, lands, and premises to the use of the said trustees, who should yearly, for ever, receive and faithfully dispose of the rents and issues towards the relief of such poor, aged, needy, or impotent people who should live within the town of Manchester, aided by the judgment and discretion of the boroughreeve and the two constables of Manchester, taking unto them as an assistant, yearly for ever, one of the churchwardens of the said parish who should happen to live in the town. The trustees to let the messuages and lands to the best advantage, year by year, and to pay the rents to the said boroughreeve, two constables, and churchwarden on the feast of St. James the Apostle, and the purification of the blessed Virgin Mary, to be by them distributed, according to their discretion, to the poor as aforesaid, to commence from and after the first year next ensuing the death of the said George Clarke, and so from year to year for ever. He appointed John Dawson, gent., and Gerard Simpkin of Manchester to give seizin of the premises to the trustees, also provided for the continuation of the trust, and appointed that the accounts should be yearly audited at the Michaelmas court leet of the manor of Manchester. His friends present at the execution of this deed were Thomas Johnson, James Lightbourne, Richard Lomax, jun., and George Pendleton. (*Lanc. Charit.*, Chetham Libr.)

The commissioners for charitable uses, in pursuance of an inquisition taken at Wigan 5th March, 1683-4, before William Daniell, esq., Peter Adlington, esq., Samuel Andrewes, and William Patten, gent., and confirmed, on the motion of Mr. Yates, counsel for the inhabitants of Manchester and the feoffees, obtained a decree of the court of chancery of the county palatino of Lancaster, dated 16th July, 1684, and signed by sir John Otway (vice-chancellor of the Duchy), whereby it was ordered that the then trustees, John Johnson, gent., Michael Dickinson, gent., Oswald Mosley, esq., John Hartley, esq., Thomas Lancashire, gent., Richard Fox, gent., Samuel Dicconson, gent., and Edward Bootle, gent., and their successors should have power to dispose, by lease, of the said premises for twenty-one years and no longer, without fine, but upon an improved yearly rent. It appeared that the farmers, having so short a term in the lands, were unwilling to improve the same, and that consequently the estate had grown barren and ruinous, and the poor did not receive the maintenance intended by their benefactor. (*Ibid.*)

In 1795 an act of parliament confirmed and enlarged the powers of the trustees, and enabled them to let lands for building and other purposes. In 1806 another act of parliament was obtained, whereby it was enacted that the trustees should have power absolutely to grant the lands in Crumpsall and Tetlow in fee or to lease the same for lives or years. In 1824 John Birch, esq., James Touchet, and James Bayley of Manchester, merchants, the surviving trustees, conveyed to the use of themselves and of John Touchet of Manchester, merchant, Shakespear Phillips of Barlow hall, esq., the rev. John Clowes of Broughton hall, one of the fellows of the collegiate church, Edward Loyd of Manchester, banker, Edward Jeremiah Lloyd of Manchester, barrister-at-law, Thomas Heywood of Salford, banker, and Samuel Bayley, John Bradshaw, Gilbert Winter, Jeremiah Fielding, and Hugh Hornby Birley, all of Manchester, merchants, and their heirs, all the then remaining residue of the said trust estate. The income of the charity amounted, in 1636, to about 100*l.* per annum, and in 1826, to more than 1,200*l.* per annum, and its receipts have probably since increased.

It is almost a matter of wonder how Mr. Clarke should have been daily a devout frequenter of the prayers in the collegiate church, and a profitable hearer of sermons there, when the rejection of church principles, the sacrilegious neglect of the fabric, and the disorderly conduct of the clergy during the first half of the seventeenth century are considered. Anything more disastrous than the state of the college, its services, and clergy, could not be conceived. Two things appear to have been entirely overlooked by these puritanical ecclesiastics — the spiritual welfare of the laity and the prosperity of the corporation. They had neither the wisdom to rule, nor the prudence to reform, the church. From the visitations of the bishops and their officials we discover an unwritten chapter on the state of the church in Manchester, at least during George Clarke's lifetime, and there is more than conjectural proof that he was in every respect the "worthy" Churchman, which Mr. Richard Johnson, the regular and orthodox fellow of the college, who personally knew him, so felicitously described him to Dr. Fuller. In 1604 Dr. John Dee, the warden, was reported to the bishop as being "noe Preacher," which may either convey the meaning that he did not preach at all, being sometimes styled "esquire," or that he was not an eloquent man in the pulpit, or what is more probable, did not come up to the Puritan standard. The learned doctor's quarrels and squabbles with the members of the chapter were a source of public scandal. (See his *Diary*, p. 63.) In the same year (1604) Mr. Ralph Kyrke, one of the chaplains, had numerous and specific articles exhibited against him before Lloyd, bishop of Chester, by the parishioners of Manchester. Amongst other grave charges, the visitor of the college was informed that Kyrke " omitted dyvers Praiers att Service commanded by the Book of Common Praier, and devysed prayers on his own heade;" also "in Baptism he dyd not observe the book of common praier by signing with the sign of the cross, and if anie of the parties that came with the Chyld to be baptised or any other dyd request him to make the sign of the Crosse, he asked them whether they would have a Black, a Redd, a Blewe, or a Headlesse Crosse, and such other contemptible words;" also "he Chrystened chyldren without Godfathers or Godmothers, or the use of the surplice, which hee preacheth is but "a ragg of the Pope and a mightie heresie in the Church," and that "he that mayntayned yt could not be saved;" also that "he would not allow divers of the Parishioners who had helped the Parish Clerk to read verse for verse with the Curate for fourtie years last paste and more, in the Morning Service, so to do, but openly commanded them to hold their peace." In July of the following year Mr. Kyrke, his wife, and three children were swept away by "the Plague." (*Lanc. MSS.*, vol. xxii. pp. 122–4.) In 1607 Mr. Oliver Carter, B.D., one of the fellows, a learned man, an acute theologian, and a favourite preacher, was nevertheless accused to the bishop of being "a common Sollicitor in temporall causes." (*Ibid.*, p. 132.) In 1608, October 11, Dr. Dee was accused of "not keeping the Chancel in sufficient repaire," nor "the body of the Church," and Mr. Bourne, another fellow, and Mr. Learoyde, a chaplain, "for administering the Communion to dyvers persons sittinge." (*Ibid.*, p. 186.) A little before this time George Dutton, schoolmaster of Trafford, had preached in Manchester church, "being an Excommunicated person," and Mr. John Buckley, chaplain, a popular preacher and a man of considerable influence, had suffered him so to preach, whilst Mr. Robert Barber, clerk, "could not reade the Prayers distinctlye." In 1609 the bishop of Chester enjoined Mr. W. Bourne, B.D., the fellow above named, "not to administer the Sacrament unlesse in his Surplice *sub pœnâ juris.*" (*Ibid.*, p. 126.) It had been proved before the archbishop of York, in 1595, that none of the fellows, ministers or choristers, "doe weare Surplices in tymes of Praier and ministration of the Sacrament," and that many of the parishioners thought the proceeding both "undecent and offensive in such a great Collegiate Church." (*Ibid.*, p. 132.) It was again shewn at a visitation, in 1611, that Mr. Bourne, the fellow, did "not weare the Surplice and Hood, nor had he read divine service in the church of Manchester since 25th September, 1608, nor administered either of the Sacraments these viii. monthes." (*Ibid.*) In 1622, through the default of Dr. Murray, the warden, "the roof of the Quier was farre out of repayre and in greate danger of fallinge." Mr. Bourne and Mr. Baker, two of the fellows, still refused to wear the surplice, whilst Mr. Tacey and Mr. Learoyde, the chaplains, daily violated the rubrics and scornfully refused to read the canons. (*Ibid.*, p. 188.) In 1630 and 1633 Dr. Murray, the warden, Mr. Bourne, and Mr. Daniel Baker were again prosecuted for divers violations of the ordinances of the church and of the collegiate charter. In the latter year Bourne was suspended, and in 1635 the warden was also suspended, and subsequently deprived. The funds of the corporation were badly administered, the building ruinous, and all the clergy, with the exception of Mr. Richard Johnson, irregular and self-willed. They determined to be fettered by no rules and to submit to no recognized authority, notwithstanding their obligation of canonical obedience. (*Ibid.*, p. 134.) Amongst the numerous and various presentments of the parishioners for breaches of church order and good morals, the name of George Clarke never occurs; but he had doubtless heard of "the wyfe of the Deanesgate," in 1590, calling one of the churchwardens "a pratinge jackey," and saying "she would talke and aske him noe leave," when he reproved her "for talking in Service tyme;" and he knew "Richard Browne of Manchester, cobler, who was vehementlie suspected to have twoe wives, and to be of that secte of the famelie of Love." He also would know Edward Pycroft, a stout maintainer of the "olde wayes," who went out of Manchester church at service time, in September, 1608, and being admonished to return again, refused, "alleging, he would not heare Mr. Bourne," the friend of John Knox. (*Ibid.*, p. 186.) And, as George Clarke was a churchwarden, he had doubtless reproved "Robert Leach and several others, who on the 13th August 1622 joyned wth those y^t began to Singe the Psalm before the Organes played, and singing in a contrarie tune to the Organes, caused confusion in the Church," so that the Parishioners complained at the chancellor's visitation, and also at the same time brought up Thomas Robinson, "who sayd that Raphe Lownde was damned for blowing the organes," in Manchester church. (*Ibid.*, p. 188.) And he had probably heard of "Margaret Hey presented to the Court for sleeping in the Church att praier and sermon,"—of Margaret Otwise "for dyppynge a chyld in the Fonte after itt was baptized,"—of Thomas Goulden, who "buryed his chyld without the Minister," and of John Thompson "for dytchinge upon St. Michael's daye." (*Ibid.*, p. 196.) And notwithstanding all these scandals, George Clarke was "a daily frequenter of prayers and a hearer of sermons," although he did not appoint any of the clergy the trustees of his charity to the poor; but a couple of years before his death, the miserable feuds and discords of half a century were quelled for a season, first by the dissolution and then by the re-founding of the college. There was, however, no disendowment, confiscation or spoliation. The spiritual welfare of the parishioners was secured, the tenure of the endowment regulated, and the rights of the clergy and their life interests confirmed. A new charter, granted by the king, was obtained by archbishop Laud, who surmounted many difficulties, and accomplished the arduous undertaking at the instigation of the rev. Richard Johnson, supported by the wisdom and pecuniary liberality of Humphrey Chetham, esq., neither of them half-hearted men, but both of them influenced by George Clarke's benevolent spirit, and, like him, "just, temperate, and frugal," and always devout and consistent members of the English church. Their constant prayer for Manchester church—"Destroy it not; for a blessing is in it"—was ultimately heard, and prevailed.

Little is known of George Clarke's family. His marriage with ——, daughter of Edmund Gee, gent., connected him with the Chethams and Mosleys, Pendletons and Worsleys, Tippings and Marlers, all at that time largely engaged in merchandise and commerce, and the heads of the principal families in Manchester. In 1625 Mr. George Clarke was the senior constable, and in 1629 the boroughreeve of the town. He also occurs as a juror of the court leet of the manor (*Manchester Court Leet Records*, pp. 172, 177), so that he filled the highest and most responsible civic offices of the town in which he dwelt. His wife's relations were of good position, and wealthy. Three brothers of her family were well beneficed in the Church, and it was remembered long after the event, that they had all preached in Manchester on the same day. (*Newcome's Autobiog.*, vol. i., p. 90.) Mr. George Clarke had been, like his personal friend and neighbour Humphrey Chetham, an industrious and provident man, who, by attending to his business had acquired a moderate competency, and having no children, devoted it to benevolent purposes. The world, it may be, judged him harshly, and perhaps posterity would have judged him more favourably had he made a more liberal provision for his widow. There seems to have been no mortuary monument to his memory on the walls of the church, but a small and humble memorial grave stone, once forming part of the pavement, was found a few years ago, during some excavations, by Mr. John Owen of Manchester, a diligent antiquary, outside the entrance of the south porch, and near the south-western angle of St. George's chapel; but it has now disappeared. The following is the fragmentary inscription; the lettering defaced, the date gone, and the whole nearly illegible :

```
HERE : LIET
THE : BODY :
GEORGE : CL
KE : WHO : D
TED : OVT :
THIS : WOR
HE : TWE
FIRST : D
```

The name of his widow was not recorded, and their surviving friends appear to have studied economy in their sepulchral record. In the *Register Book of Burials* is this brief entry: "Mr. George Clarke of Manchester, Octob' 24 1637." *R.*]

LADY DOROTHY LEIGH, 1639.

Original Funeral Certificates of the North in Coll. Arms, No. 61.

THE Lady Dorothy Leigh dyed at Worsley in the county of Lancaster vpon the 4th day Aprill 1639 and was interred in Eccles church in the sayd county.

Shee was daughter to Sr Richard Egerton of Ridley in the county of Chester Kt and did marry tow husbands: first she married Richard Brereton of Tatton in the County of Chester Esquier and by him had yssue Richard who dyed yonge: To her second husband she married Sʳ Peter Leigh of Lyme in the sayd county knight but by him she had noe yssue.

This Certyficate was taken at Worsley aforesayd vpon the 14th day of Aprell 1639 by Randle Holme of the Citty of Chester gent. deputy to the office of Armes and was certyfied under the hand of Peter Egerton of Shaw in the County of Lancaster Esqʳ nephew and one of the Executors to the defuncte.

PETER EGERTON.

A pedigree of Egerton of Ridley may be found in Ormerod's *Cheshire*, vol. ii. p. 162, by which it appears that she married Richard Brereton of Tatton, 28th April 1572; and in the same work is a pedigree of Legh of Lyme, where her marriage with sir Peter Legh is also mentioned, but it is not given in the pedigree of Legh entered at the Visitation of 1664.

The Egertons of Ridley descended from Philip Egerton of Egerton, who married Margery, daughter of William Mainwaringe of Ightfeld, whose descendants were registered at the Visitation of Cheshire, 1580. *K*.

[The will, codicil, and inventory of dame Dorothy Legh of Worsley are amongst the *Lancashire and Cheshire Wills*, 3rd portion, pp. 201-12, CHET. SER. The will is full of interesting domestic and family information. Richard Brereton, esq., of Worsley and Tatton, the first husband of this lady, having lost his only child in 1575, and dying himself on the 17th December, 1598, settled his large estates on his wife's illegitimate brother, sir Thomas Egerton, afterwards the lord chancellor Ellesmere, and ancestor of the earls and dukes of Bridgewater; but a caveat was entered at York, 22nd December, 1598, against the probate of Mr. Brereton's will, and some litigation followed, but the devise was established (*Lanc. MSS.*, vol. xxvii., p. 21), and the estates are now held by the noble representative of the Egertons, the earl of Ellesmere. Lady Legh appears to have adopted Thomas, the younger grandson of the lord chancellor. She erected a large table tomb with whole-length recumbent figures of her first husband and herself, in the year 1600, and the same still remains in the Worsley chapel, within Eccles church, where she was buried on the 11th April, 1639. *R*.]

SIR GILBERT IRELAND, 1675.

Original Funeral Certificates of the North in Coll. Arms, No.55.

SIR Gilbert Ireland of the Hutt in the County palatine of Lancaster K*t*: one of the deputy Leiut: for the said county dyed at Bewsey neere Warringtõ: the 30th of Aprill Año 1675 and was buried at Hale in the said county of Lancaster.

The said S*r* Gilbert Ireland married Margaret the onely daughter and heire of Thomas Ireland of Bewsey in the county Palatine of Lancaster Esq*r* but died without any issue, she surviving him.

This certificate was taken by Randle Holme of the Citty of Chester gent: under the hand of the Lady Ireland, Relict of the defuncte.

MARGARET IRELAND.

DAME Margarett Ireland the Relict of S*r* Gilbert Ireland of Hutt and Bewsey in the county of Lancaster K*t* died at Bewsey y*e* first of July Año 1675 and was Buryed at Hale in the County of Lancaster. She was the onely daughter and heire of Thomas Ireland of Bewsey Esq*r*: she died without issue.

This certificate was taken by Randle Holme of the citty of Chester gent: under the hand of Thomas Cooke gent: one of the Execut*rs* of the said Lady Ireland.

THOS: COOKE.

The pedigree of Ireland was recorded at the visitation of co. Lancaster in 1665, by sir Gilbert Ireland, who was then aged 41, deducing his descent from Thomas Ireland of the Hutt and Hale, co. Lancaster, who married Margaret, daughter of sir Richard Bold of Bold, knt. Sir Gilbert is described of Hutt, Hale and Bewsey, and married as above stated. His sister Eleanor, became one of his coheirs, and was married at Ormskirk to Edward Aspinwall of Aspinwall, near Ormskirk, by whom she had issue. John Blackburne of Orford, F.R.S. and M.P. for co. Lancaster, one of her descendants and representatives, recorded his pedigree in 1804. The family is now represented by John Ireland Blackburne of Hale, esq. There are pedigrees of the Irelands of the Hutt, and also of Lydiate, in Gregson's *Fragments of Lanc. K.*

[Sir Gilbert Ireland, son and heir of John Ireland of Hutt and Hale, esq., by his wife Elizabeth, daughter of sir Thomas Hayes, knt., lord mayor of London, was born on the 8th April, 1624. His father died in the 3rd year of Charles I., 1628, and his grandfather, sir Gilbert Ireland, on the 8th April, 1626, on the day when his future representative and namesake had attained his second year. The grandfather was knighted by the king at Lathom house in 1617, and was high sheriff of the county in 1622. His will is dated 30th January, 1625-6. (*Lanc. MSS.*, vol. xxvii., p. 139.)

Gilbert Ireland married Margaret, sole daughter and heiress of Thomas Ireland of Bewsey, esq. (see *ante*, p. 49), when the large estates of the two sons of sir John Ireland of Hutt and Hale, living in the latter part of the fifteenth century, became again united, by virtue of a settlement made by Mr. Ireland of Bewsey, in the year 1637. Gilbert Ireland was high sheriff of the county in 1648.

During the commonwealth he espoused the popular cause, and Cromwell made him governor of Chester. In 1654 he was returned as one of the four members for the county of Lancaster, and in 1656 filled the same office, being described at that time as "Colonel Gilbert Ireland." (Baines' *Hist.*, vol. i., p. 319.) He assisted Charles, earl of Derby, in his petition to the house for redress (*Moore Rental*, p. 139, App. CHET. SER.), and in 1658-9 sat in Richard Cromwell's parliament as burgess for Liverpool. He was one of that numerous class of presbyterians who, after diligently achieving the overthrow of Charles the First, occupied themselves in restoring his son. (*Norris Papers*, p. 20.) As a reward for his loyalty or subserviency he received the honour of knighthood in the year 1660, and, after the restoration, seems to have enjoyed the political interest and support of Charles, earl of Derby. He was appointed one of the earl's deputy-lieutenants in 1665 (*Lanc. MSS.*, vol. xi.), and was also in the commission of the peace for the county. In the year 1660 he was returned to the new parliament for

Liverpool, along with the hon. William Stanley. A dissolution taking place shortly afterwards, he was again returned for the same borough, in the Stanley interest, in the following year, and retained his seat until his death, which Mr. Thomas Heywood, on the authority of Baines (vol. iv., p. 147), erroneously says, occurred in the year 1678. (*Norris Papers*, p. 20.) Gregson observes that sir Gilbert impoverished himself by his Liverpool elections. (*Fragmts.*, p. 102.) In 1665, in accordance with his altered principles, he certified to Dugdale, with the leaders of the royalist party, that Theophilus Howarth of Howarth, esq., in the parish of Rochdale, "had, with great courage, fidelity, and constancy, adhered to his most illustrious, serene, and sacred Majesty King Charles the first, of late and blessed memory, and for his loyalty had been a great sufferer both in estate and person, and had been serviceable to his then Majesty's faithful friends and subjects in those late disloyal and unhappy times," which led to an allusive augmentation of the armorial bearings of the said Howarth, who would hardly have applied to sir Gilbert for his testimonium in the late "disloyal times." (*Lanc. MSS.*, vol. xi., p. 129.) He had perhaps never been a very sincere or zealous presbyterian, and at the restoration conformed to the church. He was, however, hotly opposed, like his patron, Charles, earl of Derby, to the views of the Roman catholic church, and "talked of popery coming in," which Pepys, in 1662, said, "all the fanatiques doe." He is often named with respect in the unpublished *Letters and Correspondence* of his excellent kinsman, Richard Legh of Lyme, esq., M.P. (*Lanc. MSS.*) Feb. 26, 1669, Mr. Legh writes from London to his wife at Lyme: "Yesterday we read the Bill for the King's Supply and upon Monday 'twill be read again — nobody opposeth it now. A strict Bill against Fanaticks is preparing. We have met severall times about it, and have it ready now to bring into the house." On the 6th November, 1673, he again writes: "There was such burning of the Pope last night. Sir Anthony Cope had a barrell of pitch and a Mawment of Straw (one of Downes Legh's 'John Obetts'), that had a triple Crown, lawne sleaves, a cope, and severall fripperies, like to his Holiness at Rome, which was sett in the Barrel of Pitch, and a linke fir'd, and stuck i'th' reare of itt, which gave fire, and a thousand people, I doe believe, were spectators. My brother Jack and I walked an houre by the light of it. It was set in the higher end of the Square. The Lady Devonshire and the Lady Southampton had each a great fire there.

My Father [in-law, Sir Tho. Chicheley] another; and a sad accident had like to have been, for the boys were charging their guns in the Hall, and a pound of gunpowder took fire in the Hall window, and did noe more hurt then burn the old Porter's Beard (who came not long since) and the haire which he had, in a most magnificent manner. Sir Gilbert Ireland enjoyed the sport." On the 6th February, 1674-5, sir Gilbert was at Hutt, keeping up unbounded hospitality, and Mr. Legh was engaged to dine with him on the following day, having dined with sir William Gerard, at Garswood, on the preceding day, and was afterwards to proceed to Croxheath. On the 27th April, 1675, Mr. Legh again writes from London: "To day the House sate till almost foure, and we were obliged to be at a Committee before six. The news of Parliament and a Gazette I have herewith sent — thou wilt see how they screwe, and another is expected to come on. One thing pleaseth me that I see, the House is pretty calme (though severe), and I hope the conclusion may end well, for the malicious party are broke. I have visited the good Lord Archbishop of York, who is concerned as deeply in theirs as the youngest in our House, and when, yesterday, the Lords were so warme they moved, at 4 in the afternoon, to adjourn their Debate, which still continues upon the Test, they believing the Bishops, being old men, would have been glad of that recesse. The old Lads, however, mov'd to stick to it, and at nine or ten at night they voted the Test to be reduced into a Bill. Methinks the actions of . . . .[35] and these days are now upon the Stage, and the violent Presbyterians and Papists goe hand in hand in that house. . . . . Sir Gilbert Ireland's worst fears seem likely to come to pass. . . . ."

His days, however, were numbered, as, on the 30th April, 1675 he expired at Bewsey, at the age of 51, having been elected mayor of Liverpool in the preceding year, so that he was not in the house of commons during these debates, and died in his mayoralty. (*Moore Rental*, p. 132.) He is said to have been a man of haughty temper and stately demeanour. From excessive drinking and extravagant expenditure of money, his electioneering proved fatal to his purse and injurious to his health. (Gregson's *Fragments*, Harland's Ed., p. 102.) On the 8th May Mr. Legh writes from London: "The Lords are still very high about their privileges, and now we have a new quarrell, betwixt a member of ours (one S' John Fagg), who was summoned

---

[35] A few words in cypher.

to their Bar upon a suite, and the two Houses are to have Conferences. This is a brave bone cast betwixt the two Houses at this critical time. In short, the Papist and Presbyterian joyne heartily against the Church of England. Yesterday we had a Letter from the King in answer to our Addresse, wth the Reasons against Lauderdale. — 'Tis a hard pull they put upon the King, to gratify their lust in every thing, and nobody can tell when they are pleas'd. Some believe they carry with this height to force a Dissolution. This morning the King sent us another Answer, by Secretary Coventry, to the Addresse for recalling his subjects out of France. He told us there was but a few, and those were established at the time he concluded the peace with Holland, and desir'd he might not intrench upon that, and, for the future, he promised his Proclamation should come out, that noe more should goe. This, too, would not downe without further consideration, soe 'twas deferr'd till Monday — the consideration thereof. As yet nothing is done either for King or Country. . . . ." On the 10th May Mr. Legh again writes from London: "I tould you in my last that Lyrpool election was likely to be warmly contested, but I have made no promises. Sr Gilbert, wth all his endeavour for the welfare of that place, is now accused of serving the times, and some minions, I say not underlings, who profess'd to be his friends, now spitefully add, his own turns too. Had these dar'd to say soe much in his time, they would have had a torturing racke, and would have been rightly thought the falsest and unthankfullest of mortals. Thou knowest one of 'em, him that hath his portion in this life, for he said to thee, his heaven was here, and no wonder he devises to make his paradise as dainty as he can; but the lines and levels of his ambition and bitter girds ought not to concur to the damage of Sr Gilbert's honour, for the grave covers him, and I know his ways were of another fashion. But what foul dunghills malice and envy doe belch out. Sr Gilbert look'd death in the face without dread, and mett the blessed Master he always profess'd to serve (God knows *how*), as Legh Bowdon assured me, with sweet content and undaunted spirit, and my worst wish for his detractors is, that they may doe the same. . . . ."

At the latter part of sir Gilbert Ireland's life the Roman catholics were still striving for the ascendancy, and he supported the Test act, and vindicated the penal laws, which were so objectionable to Dryden, and the party to which he had attached himself. After the death of sir Gilbert, the Declaration of Liberty of Conscience was published, and the "Hind and Panther" appeared. The poet represented the church of Rome as a milk-white Hind, always in peril from the church of England Panther, the Presbyterian Wolf, the Independent Bear, the Anabaptist Boar, and the Socinian Fox, all glaring fiercely at her. The burden of the poem was to induce the Dissenters to make common cause with the Roman catholics against the church of England. This, it will be observed, was well known to intelligent men like Richard Legh and sir Gilbert Ireland, and, notwithstanding their firm adherence to Charles the Second's general policy, they were scrupulous in their support of the independence of the English church. James the Second's object was to further these long concealed views of the Roman catholic party, and, as Macauley observes, to overpower the Anglican church by forming a coalition of sects against her. On the 2nd January 1678-9 Mr. Legh writes from London: "Some say the King is very uneasy since the Prorogation. I praye God spare his life. Here is the saddest Christmas ever was known. Now they begin to say this (Oates' Plot) was only a contrivance of Dr. Tillotson and some such. The woman in Long Acre I saw, too, last night, and she calls the Priests 'poor creatures' and 'wretches' 'they never think any body any harm, and as for Oates and Bedlow, one is mad, and the other has been burnt i'th' hand. Now 'tis seen why they durst not write.' This day I dined at Mr. Attorney's wth Sir Thomas [Chicheley, chancellor of the duchy of Lancaster] and Dr. Tillotson. I was invited to Sir Robert Carr's where I have been this even. and found the Lord Derby and the two Lyrpool Burgesses, and have left them all at Cards, with Tom Cholmley and the ladies. They goe to morrow to Sir John Bennett's twelve miles off . . . ." (*Lanc. MSS.*)

Sir Gilbert Ireland died in involved circumstances, and assigned by will his large estates in trust for the payment of his debts, empowering his trustees to lease his Lancashire and to sell his Cheshire property. It seems, however, that he afterwards sequestered his estates for twenty or thirty years, until his circumstances were discharged, and left each of his sisters £180 a year for life. (Gregson's *Fragments*, p. 202.) He was buried in his own Chapel at Hale, in the parish of Childwall, and a blue marble flat stone covers his remains, on which is incised: "ULTIMUS DOMÛS. FIAT VOLUNTAS DEI."

His two surviving sisters Eleanor and Martha succeeded to the annuity charged on his paternal estates, whilst Bewsey passed under the deed of settlement of Thomas Ireland, esq., dated 1637 (see *ante*, p. 49,) to his nephew Richard Atherton of Atherton, esq., M.P., after the death of Margaret, lady Ireland, which occurred two months subquent to her husband's premature decease.

With this lady expired an old and honoured Lancashire name, which centuries had invested with popular regard, and which she found, and for any thing which appears to the contrary left, unsullied. Unfortunately, however, the Irelands have left no public monuments to prove that they did not live for themselves alone. *R.*]

SIR THOMAS GERRARD, 1601.

Original Funeral Certificate of the North. State Paper Office.[36]

Sr Thomas Gerrard of the Bryne in the co. of Lancaster Knight, deceased on the —— of September anno 1601 and was Interred in Wynwick Church in his Chaple in the said County on the xxviijth of October A^o predict.

He maried Elizabeth eldest daughter and one of the heyres of Sr John Port of Etwall in Derbyshire. They haue yssue Thomas Gerrard Esq. theire sonne and heyre John Gerrard 2^d sonne Dorothy Gerrard Mary Gerrard and Martha Gerrard.

The said Thomas Gerrard sonne of Sr Thomas hath maryed Cyseley daughter to Walter Maney Esq. and by her hath yssue Thomas Gerrard sonne and heyre John Gerrard 2^d sonne Elizabeth eldest daughter Fraunces 2^d daughter.

Dorothy eldest daughter to Sr Thomas maryed to Ed. Peckam Esq. and have yssue, Mary 2^d daughter to Sr Thomas hath maryed John Jenisonne Esq^o and hath yssue.

[36] Published also in *Miscellanea Genealogica et Heraldica*, by J. J. Howard, LL.D., F.S.A. *Part* ii., *p.* 46, *Oct.*, 1866.

Martha Gerrard youngest daughter to Sr Thomas maryed Michell Jeneson brother to John aforesaid.

This wo^{ll} Knight deceased beareth for his first Coate the field argent a Saltyer gules. The 2^d Azur a lyon Rampant or, crowned or. The 3 Azur a lyone Rampant argent. The 4th argent vpon a bend azur 3 staggs heads cabesed or. The 5th quarterly Indented gules & or. The 6th sa. a Cheueron engr. betweene 3 owlets ar. The 7th argent vpon a cheveron gules 3 bezants. The 8 gules a bend argent. The 11th g. a sythe argent. All these Coates I fynd quartered in the glasse wyndow in his Chaple at the Bryne which weer boarne by his ancester in an° 1518.

Tho. Gerard.

In this funeral certificate, omitted in its proper place, three generations of the Gerard family are mentioned.

The first is sir Thomas Gerard, knight, who died in the year 1601. He was the head of one of the great Lancashire families, and was descended "of gentle blood," being the son of Thomas Gerard of Bryn, esq., by his wife Jane, daughter of sir Peter Legh of Lyme, knt. (Marr. Cov., dated 18th July, 9 Hen. VIII., *Lanc. MSS.*, vol. xxxviii., p. 443), and was born, according to computation, about the year 1525. I would not desecrate the grave, to adopt a remark of lord Macaulay, nor dig up the skeletons of the departed only to mutilate and insult them, but truth will not be injured by stating that this son was not trained in a happy or domestic home. His father knew nothing of letters, and spent his time in the too fashionable amusements of his age, being addicted to gallantry, hunting, drinking, and carousing, and yet it could not be said of him, as of the independent and magnanimous lord Marmion,

———————— he scarce received
For Gospel what the Church believed,

as he continued attached to the creed in which he had been educated. He committed, however, a great social outrage upon his young wife, the daughter of sir Peter Legh, one of the most influential of the Lancashire and Cheshire territorial families. In the year 1543 he was "con-

vented," under the style and title of "Syr Thomas Gerard of the
Brynne, Knyght," before the king's commissioners for divers causes in
the north, and sundry allegations were brought against him, his general
conduct being considered injurious in example to his son Thomas
(whose funeral certificate is here printed), and prejudicial to the church
and commonweal. As a curious feature of the state of morals in Lancashire about the time of the Reformation, some of the statements made
in this case may be here given, nor was it at that period by any means
a singular case. National manners were reflected by national amusements; but with the Reformation the manners gradually improved,
whilst the sports of the field became more restricted to the sterner sex.

"1 *June*. xxxv. Hen. viii. 1543. At which daye forasmoche as it
appearyd to ye Kynges Comissoners that Thomas Gerard of the Bryne
hath kept a Concubyne and lyved in Adulterye. And that the disagree-
ment betwyxt him and hys wyfe hath bene the cose and originall
grounde thereof. And yt further appeareth to the s^d Comissioners that
by medyacion of fryndes and for desyr to plese god the same Thomas
and hys wyfe wyll cohabyt and gree agayne togeder: It is Ordered that
from hensforth the sayd Thomas Gerard of th'one ptye and Jane Gerard
and Peers Legh her brother (who had also married Margaret daughter
of Thomas Gerard of the Bryn) of th'other ptye shall not only be
faythfull loving and harty fryndes together But that also the said
Thomas and Jane shall forget and forgive all fawtes trespasses and
offences by hys sayd wyfe heretofore comytted and ye sayd Thomas in
lyke mañer, and they shall knyt in hartys wth faythfull love a new and
pfecte Matrymonye. And the said Peers Legh and his wife Margaret
and the sayd Jane Gerard the iii. daye of Julye next comyng shall
lovyngly with free and gentle harts come together to Wyndlishaw and
there Hunt and make merry with the said Thomas Gerard and his
frynds and that the morrow after that is to say the iiii. daye of July
the said Thomas Gerard and Jane his wyfe shall goe agayne to Hunt
and make merry with the sayd Peers Legh at Bradley and then return
with his sayd wyfe to the Bryn, or whither him pleaseth, and cohabit
with his sayd wyfe. . . . . And if any breach or disagree-
ment doe chaunce again betwixt the sayd Thomas and his wyfe they
shall upon proofe thereof immediately pay to the sayd Peers Legh
vi*l*. xiii*s*. iiii*d*. for costs and charges he hath sustayned heretofore. And

above all, the Comissioners doe order that from hensforth the sayd Thomas shall kepe no carnal accompanye with hys olde Concubyne nowther take no newe one unto him. And that the Penanuce for his misdemenors heretofore due and condygne shalbe further respettyd tyll tryall of his Amendment............ The said Thomas also entered into obligatory Covenants with the King........." (*Lanc. MSS.*, vol. xxii., p. 170.) On the 12th August, 1537, he presented Mr. John Harper, master of decrees, to the rectory of Brindle, which he had recovered by a process at law from sir William Cavendish (*Reg. Lichf.*), and in 1549, he settled the advowson on Margery, wife of sir John Port, knt., his stepfather, erroneously called by Baines (vol. iii., p. 497) his "father-in-law." This connection, however, is not given in the Port pedigree in Bigsby's *History of Repton*. In 1553, being the high sheriff of Lancashire, he was a commissioner for the subsidy, granted in that year, along with Edward, earl of Derby (who was often in the duchy court, on matters in dispute and litigation with his late father, sir Thomas Gerard), sir Richard Molyneux of Sefton, sir Peter Legh of Lyme, sir John Holcroft of Holcroft, sir John Atherton of Atherton, and sir William Norris of Speke, knts. It may be hoped that he had become reconciled to his wife, and that they had " knyt in hartys w^h faythfull love a new and pfect matrymonye," as he rebuilt Bryn hall, in the reign of Edward the sixth and his arms, impaling those of Legh of Lyme, remained there in the last century. In the 8 and 9 Elizabeth he was M.P. for the county of Lancaster. (Baines, vol. iii., p. 641.) He died about the year 1571.

He was succeeded by his eldest son, sir Thomas Gerard, knt., whose funeral certificate is here printed. He married his kinswoman, Elizabeth, daughter and coheiress of sir John Port of Etwall, co. Derby, K.B., M.P., by his wife Elizabeth, daughter of sir Thomas Gifford of Chillington castle, co. Stafford, and with this marriage the recollection of the various unhappy disputes and lengthened litigation between sir John Port the elder, chief justice of the king's bench (and dame Margery, his second wife), with his stepson, sir Thomas Gerard, regarding his mother's claim of excessive dower, lands, and possessions within the manors of Windleshaw, Eccleston, and elsewhere in Lancashire, would pass away. (*Duch. Lanc. Records.*) Old lady Port was the grandmother of Thomas Gerard, esq., and he married her second husbadn's granddaughter. The mother of sir John Port was Jane, daughter and heiress of John Fitzherbert of Etwall, and relict of John Pole of Radbourne, co. Derby, esq. Sir John Port will always be deservedly memorable as the liberal founder, in 1557, of Repton grammar school and of the hospital of Etwall, which useful charities were incorporated by letters patent, granted in 1621, by James the first. The present trustees and patrons of these wealthy institutions are the descendants of the three daughters and coheiresses of sir John Port, viz.: 1. sir Robert Tolver Gerard, bart., in right of his ancestress, Elizabeth Port; 2. Francis, twelfth earl of Huntingdon, in right of his ancestress, Dorothy Port, who married George, fourth earl of Huntingdon (a title, unhappily, just extinct); 3. George, sixth earl of Chesterfield, in right of his ancestress, Margaret Port, who married sir Thomas Stanhope of Shelford, co. Notts, knt., M.P. (See *Hist. of Repton*, by Robert Bigsby, esq., LL.D. 4to. 1854.)

Sir Thomas Gerard filled none of the high county offices during this reign, nor did he unite with the loyal supporters of the crown in defending the queen against her enemies, foreign and domestic, and yet Baines says he distinguished himself by his zealous and disinterested service in his country's cause (vol. i., p. 559), of which, however, I have failed to discover any proof, except in his compulsory legal contributions. He was never a guest at Knowsley during the lifetime of Henry, earl of Derby, and therefore was excluded from the splendid hospitalities and receptions of that popular nobleman. (*Stanley Papers*, part ii.) He strongly maintained the creed, innovations, and accretions of the Latin church, and was twice sent to the tower on a charge, first, in 1572, of aiding the duke of Norfolk, in conjunction with the court of Rome, to depose queen Elizabeth, to liberate the queen of Scots, to elevate her to the crown, and to restore the Roman catholic religion (*Burghley Papers*, vol. ii., p. 771), and afterwards owing to his complicity in Throgmorton's conspiracy. He only obtained his own liberty by alienating the noble estate of his great-grandmother, which had descended to him from the Bromleys, to his wealthy, influential, and perhaps rapacious kinsman, sir Gilbert Gerard, M.P., at that time the attorney-general. Sir Thomas was also compelled to dispose of several manors in Leicestershire, Derbyshire, Cheshire, and Lancashire, owing to the expenses incurred by his political disaffection, and left his estates much encumbered by fines, mortgages, and other imposts. He had a natural son, who was also ill-affected to the state, and in a list of Lancashire recusants of the 10th Sept., 1586, there was one "Burton, a Preest, of the same gang, remayning wth the wyfe of Sr Thomas Gerott's base sonne, being a Fleming borne, and a very great harbourer of the ill-affected gent. in those parts. (Baines, vol. i., p. 542.) His chief allies in Lancashire were sir Thomas and sir Edward Stanley (see *ante*, p. 40), the two sons of the third earl of Derby, and one Rolleston. He left issue, as recorded in this certificate, 1. sir Thomas, 2. John, who, as a champion of the Roman catholic party, is conspicuous as one of the resolute band of men who disowned his allegiance to queen Elizabeth, rejected her supremacy, and refused to acknowledge her claim to the crown. Like the reformers of the preceding reign, he was exposed to bitter obloquy and harsh persecution, was imprisoned in the tower, and is said to have been several times tortured; but fortunately escaping from his confinement, he settled at Rheims, and, as his prison discipline had failed to shake his convictions and constancy, he became one of the founders of the Jesuits' college there. He is doubtless "the sonne of Sr Thos Gerard," who was "a person to be sought after," being suspected of implication in Babington's plot. (*Harl. MSS.* 360, quoted by Baines, vol. i., 541.) Of the daughters of sir Thomas, 1. Mary married John Jenison of Walworth, co. Durham, esq.; 2. Dorothy married Edmond, son of sir George Peckham, knt.; and 3. Martha married Michael Jenison, gent., brother of the said John. In 1601 sir Thomas was succeeded by his eldest son, also named in this funeral certificate. He was born about the year 1557. In 1584-5 he accompanied Henry, earl of Derby, on his grand embassage to France, and in the next year he was elected M.P. for Lancaster, being a deputy-lieutenant and justice of the peace for the county. He is memorable as having been the warm personal friend and constant companion of Ferdinando, fifth earl of Derby, and they were probably two of the most accomplished and genial young men in the county. Mr. Payne Collier has shown, from the *Registers of the Stationers' Company*, how generally the poets of the time lamented the death of the latter, although several of their ephemeral productions have perished; and Mr. Thomas Gerard is frequently named as a guest at Knowsley and Lathom house. (*Stanley Papers*, part ii.)

On Sunday, 25th November, 1587, Mr. John Dudley and Mr. Gerard arrived at Knowsley (whilst the earl was "at the Court"), on a visit to Ferdinando lord Strange. On the following Thursday they rode to Lathom, where they remained until the Tuesday, when they again returned to Knowsley. After a short stay Mr. Gerard went to Bryn, as on the Monday next following he and his wife again visited lord and lady Strange, and staid until the end of the week, enjoying the profuse hospitalities and fashionable amusements of "the Northern Court." (pp. 43-44.) On Wednesday, 20th January, 1587-8, the day after the earl had gone to London, lord Strange, lord Dudley, lady Compton (sister of lady Strange), Mr. John Dudley, Mr. Legh, and Mr. Gerard, went to the said Mr. Gerard's house at the Brynn (p. 47), and on the next day Mr. Gerard and his wife returned to Knowsley with lord Strange. On the day following Mr. Gerard departed. (*Ibid.*) In Dec., 1593, Thomas Gerard of the Bryn, gent., and Ferdinando, earl of Derby, were elected governors of Blackburn grammar school, at that time a great protestant institution, and each of them gave "in benevolence" to the school fund xx*s*. In 1616 sir Thomas Gerard, bart., gave to the same fund xxii*s*.; and in 4th Car., 1628, sir Thomas Gerard and nine other knights and baronets were governors of the same school, one of its early governors and principal patrons being "Thomas Gerard, Esq., H.M. Attorney-General." (*Lanc. MSS.*, Blackburn School.) On the 17th April, 1603, being one of the loyal Lancashire gentlemen who signed the congratulatory address from the county to the king at Wigan, he and his eldest son received the honour of knighthood at Grimston, near York, on the 31st March, from James the first, then on his progress to London to take possession of the crown (Baines, vol. i., p. 565); and on the 22nd May, 1611, he (the father) was created a baronet on the first day of the institution of the order, and had the singular favour of a gratuitous patent in consideration of the losses sustained by his father in behalf of Mary queen of Scots, and there is reason to conclude that he had before this time renounced his hereditary creed, and become a member of the church of England. Bishop Challoner records an instance of his great harshness, in forcing his Roman catholic brother, Mr. Nicholas Gerard, to the protestant church, and placing him opposite the minister during the service. (*Mem. Mission. Priests*, vol. ii., p. 130.) In July and August, 1612, he was actively employed in taking the depositions of witnesses against a poor old witch, at Windle, and he was determined that the hundred of West Derby should have its witch as well as other parts of the country. A more melancholy tissue of absurd and incoherent accusations against the prisoner, says Mr. Crossley, it would not be easy to find. She was hanged, from all that appears, because one person was suddenly "pinched on her thigh, as she thought, with four fingers and a thumb," and because another was "sore pained with a great warch in his bones." (Potts' *Discov. of Witchcraft*, p. 44, note, CHET. SER.) In 1614 he was returned to parliament by sir Peter Legh of Lyme, for the nomination borough of Newton, but appears only to have sat in one session. (Baines' *Hist.*, vol. iii., p. 646.) In 1617 he was one of the Lancashire gentlemen who met the king at Hoghton Tower. (Assheton's *Journal*, p. 25.) In 1623 he was M.P. for Liverpool. (Baines' *Hist.*, vol. iv., p. 146.)

In 1628 father Edmund Arrowsmith (whose mother was a daughter of Mr. Nicholas Gerard, and the niece of sir Thomas), a Jesuit priest, born at Haydock, in the parish of Winwick, in the year 1585, educated at Douay, and politically opposed to the crown and church of England, was, in pursuance of the narrow policy of the age, executed at Lancaster. (Bishop Challoner's *Mem. of Mission. Priests*, vol. ii. p. 130.) The hand of the martyr was afterwards sent to Bryn, and forms the subject of a legend, elaborated by Mr. Roby, in his second series of *Traditions of Lancashire* (vol. ii.); but he erroneously states that father Arrowsmith was executed "in the time of William the third," after "having been found guilty of a rape!" (*Ibid.*, p. 186.) The hand of sir Thomas Gerard resting on a skull in the picture which contains his portrait, painted when a young man, has some obvious reference to his religious convictions, but which, whatever they were, did not prevent lord Strange from cultivating the most intimate relations with him. (See p. 68, *ante*.)

Sir Thomas married three wives: 1. Cecily, daughter of sir Walter Mancy of Staplehurst, co. Kent., knt., by whom he had a son, sir Thomas, who died 20 Jac. I. v.p. (leaving issue eight children), and the children named in this funeral certificate; 2. he married Mary, daughter of sir John Hawes, knt., lord mayor of London, and widow, first of Mr. John Smythe, a citizen of London, and, afterwards, of sir Robert Leigh,

knt.; 3. he married Mary, daughter of William Dormer, esq., and
widow of —— Browne. He had no issue by either of these two wives.
He died in 1630, aged about 73, and his *Inq. post-mortem* was taken
6th Car. I., his grandson being found to be his heir, and the successor
to the baronetcy. Sir Thomas was buried in his chapel, which existed
in the year 1492, within Winwick church; but there is no monument
to his memory. The family had also a chantry chapel at Ormskirk.
(*Hist. Lanc. Chantries*, p. 100; *Stanley Papers*, part ii., note.) *R.*]

INDEX.

ADLINGTON, Peter, 75.
Allen, Richard, 52.
Alport lodge, Manchester, 19.
Anderson, sir Edmund, 70.
Anderton, Thurstan, 42.
———, "golden-mouthed," 67.
Andrewes, Samuel, 75.
Angier, rev. John, 55.
Anglesargh, co. Lanc., 12.
Arneshead, co. Westmoreland, 12.
Arrowsmith, Edmund, execution of, 95.
Ashaw, Mr., of the Hill, 8.
Ashton, Richard, of Croston, 48.
Aspinwall, Edward, 39, 83.
Assheton, Mr., of Chadderton, 8.
———, sir Raphe, of Whalley, 59.
Aston, sir Thomas, of Aston, 49, 50.
Atherton, George, 52.
———, John, of Atherton, 49, 51, 52, 59.
———, sir John, of Atherton, 91.
———, Richard, of Atherton, 52, 88.
———, Mr. and Mrs., 52.
Aughton, Ric., 33.
———, Mrs., 34.
Aunslowe, Mrs., 36.
Awleston, co. Lanc., 12.

BAILEY, James, 57.
——— John, of Kingsley, 29.
Baker, rev. Daniel, 78.
Banastre, —, of Bank, 50.
Banester, Ric., of Wem, 42.
Banckes, William, of Winstanley, 49.
Bankes, James, of Winstanley, 50, 52.
———, William, 50, 52.
———, Mrs., 52.
Barber, rev. Robert, 77.
Barlow family, 45–7.
———, sir Alexander, 61; notices of, 45, 46.

Barlow, Ellis, 9, 46.
———, Margaret, 52.
Barlowe, Alexander, 13.
Barnes, Tho., 52.
Barnett, Mrs., 52.
Barrow, William, 52.
Barton, Richard, of Barton, 61.
———, Robert, of Smithills, 29. 36.
———, Tho., 52.
Bate, Dr., 67.
Bayley, James, 75.
———, Samuel, 76.
Beck, Stephen, 8.
Belfield, Ralph, of Clegg hall, 46.
Bently, Mr., 52.
Berkeley, Henry lord, 17.
Beswick, Roger, 8.
Bigsby's *History of Repton*, 91, 92.
Birch, John, 75.
Birkenhead, Rawfe, 14.
Birley, Hugh II., 76.
Blackburn grammar school, 66.
Blackburne, John, 83.
Blundell, William, of Crosbie, 42.
Bold family, 58–9.
———, Richard, of Bold, 58, 82.
Doler, John, of Kingsey, 28.
Bolton en le Mores, 12.
———, Robert, 67.
Booth family, 48.
———, captain, of Stockport, 50.
——— [Bouth], John, of Barton, 47.
———, Robert, 55.
Bootle, Edward, 75.
Borton in Lonsdale, co. York, 12.
Bourne, rev. W., 77, 78.
Bradford, John, martyr, 8.
Bradley, 90.
———, John, 20.

o

INDEX.

Bradshaw, John, 51, 76.
Brereton, Richard, of Tatton, 80, 81.
——, sir Urian, of Handforth, 45, 46.
——, William, of Ashley, 46.
Brettergh family, of Brettergh-holt, notices of, 38.
——, John, 39.
—— [Bretargh], Katherine, notices of, 37–40; Latin lines on, 39.
——, Maud, 39.
——, William, 39.
Browne, Richard, cobler, 78.
Bruen, John, of Bruen Stapleford, 37, 39.
Buckley, rev. John, 77.
——, Richard, 54.
Bulkley's (Edw.) *Apologie for Religion*, 71.
Bunbery, sir Henry, of Stanney, 42.
Burials, orders respecting, 1–3.
Burscoghe, T., 21.
Butler, Edward, 50.
——, Henry, 20.
——, sir Thomas, of Bewsey, 42.
—— chapel, Warrington, 49.
Byrom, Henry, of Byrom, 51.
Byron, sir John, 66.
Bythome, co. Westmoreland, 12.

CALDWELL, John, parson of Winwick, his sermon, 64.
Canou, Dr., 67.
Carew, sir George, 66.
Carey, Mrs., 36.
Carre, Ewan, 14.
Carter, Oliver, B.D., 77.
Cartmell, co. Lanc., 20.
Caryll [Carrell], sir Thomas, 60, 61.
Case, rev. Thomas, 55.
——, Dr., 67.
Cavendish, sir William, 91.
Cecill, Thomas, earl of Exeter, 47.
Chaderton, bishop, 19, 27, 67.
Chadwicke, Adam, 35.
——, James, 35.
Challoner, bishop, 94, 95.
——, Elizabeth, 39.
——, sir Thomas, 28.
Chandos, Gray Bridges lord, 62.
Charlles, Petter, 35.
Cheek, sir Thomas, 49.
Chester, book of ships &c. in river of, 20.
Chetham, Humphrey, 74, 79.
Chicheley, sir Thomas, 85, 87.
Childwall, co. Lanc., 13.
Chorley, co. Lanc., 12.

Clarke, George, notices of, 73–80.
Claughton, co. Lanc., 12.
Clifton, Cuthbert, of Southworth, 50.
——, Thomas, of Westbye, 42.
Clowes, rev. John, 76.
Cobōne, To., 75.
Coe, rev. John, 52, 53.
Collyer, Dr., 8.
Compton, sir Henry, 3.
Cooke, Robert, clarencieux, 3.
Cope, sir Anthony, 84.
Cople, co. Lanc., 12.
Cotgrave, Hugh, Richmond herald, 4.
Cotton, sir George, of Combermere, 10.
Crowther George, 55.
Crumpsall near Manchester, 74.

DANIELL, William, 75.
Darcy, sir Henry, 3.
Danter's (John) *Lancashire's Lamentation* 66.
Davenport, sir Humphrey, 48.
Davis's (John) *Holy Roode*, 71.
Daviest, Jhon, 35.
Dawson, John, 75.
Dee, Dr. John, 76, 77.
Derby, Edward third earl of, notices of, 4–15; epitaph on, 14–5.
——, Henry fourth earl of, 63; notices of, 15–28.
——, Ferdinando fifth earl of, 93, 94; notices of, 63–9; portraits, 68; Alice his countess, 62–73.
——, William sixth earl of, 31, 60, 69.
Detheck, Nicholas, Windsor herald, 28.
Dethicke, sir Gilbert, 1.
Dicconson, Samuel, 76.
Dickenson, Michael, 75.
Dormer, William, 96.
Dormyssius, [? of] Ulster, 13.
Doughtie, Michael, 69.
Downes, John, of Wordley, 48.
Draycote [Draycort], Philip, 42, 48.
Dryden, John, 86, 87.
Dudley, John, 14, 94.
Dukenfield, James, of Hindley, 59.
Dutton, George, 77.

EGERTON, sir John, earl of Bridgwater, 62.
——, sir Thomas, lord Ellesmere, chancellor, 62, 69, 70, 71, 72, 81.
——, Philip, of Egerton, 81.
——, Peter, of Shaw.

INDEX.

Egerton, sir Richard, of Ridley, 80.
Egertons of Ridley, 81.
Eggerton, John, 14.
Elcock, Alexander, 55.
Ellis, Hugh, 69.
Etwall hospital, 92.

FAGG, sir John, 85.
Harington, William, of Worden, 13, 30; notice of, 31; Anne his wife, 34.
——, Margaret, notice of, 33.
Fielding, Jeremiah, 76.
Fitton, sir Edward, 19.
——, Mrs., 36.
Fitzherbert, John, of Etwall, 92.
Fleetwood, Richard, of Penwortham, 48.
——, William, notices of, 28–9.
Flower, William, norroy, 4.
ffogg, Jhon, 35.
Fouldrey, peel of, 20.
Fox, Richard, 75.
——, Scholastica, 39.
——, William, of Rhodes, 39.
Fuller, Dr., 76; quotation from his *Worthies*, 73–4.
Furnes, co. Lanc., 20.
ffynney, Nicholas, 13.

GARDINER, John, 52.
Gaskell, John, 74.
Gee, Edmund, 73, 79.
Gerard family, 88–96.
——, sir Gilbert, 60.
——, John, 88, 93.
——, Nicholas, 94.
——, Piers, 52.
——, sir Robert T., 68.
——, sir Thomas, 88, 91–6.
——, Thomas, of Bryn, 66, 68.
——, sir William, 85.
Gifford, sir Thomas, 91.
Gillibrownde, Tho., 14.
Gorsuch [Gossach], James, 46.
Goulden, Thomas, 79.
Greasley, sir Thomas, 45.
Griffin, John, 74.

HAREFIELD Place, Middlesex, 70, 71.
Harper, rev. John, 91.
Harrington's (sir John) *Epigrams*, quotation from, 70.
Harrison, rev. William, 39; funeral sermon by, 38.

Hartley, John, 74, 75.
Hawarden, Anne, 13.
Hawes, sir John, 95.
Hayes, sir Thomas, 83.
Heaton, Rapho, 39.
Hesketh, Bartholomew, 32, 33.
——, Gabriell, of Aughton, 30, 32.
——, Jane, notice of, 31.
——, Robert, notice of, 32.
——, Thomas, of Blackmore, notice of, 33.
——, sir Thomas, of Rufford, M.P., 51.
Hey, Margaret, 78.
Heywood, Thomas, 76, 84.
——'s (Robert), *Poems*, extract from, 25.
Hill's (Robert), *Pathway to Prayer*, 71.
Hinde's *Life* of Mrs. Brettergh, 38, 39, 40.
Hockenhall, John, of Prenton in Wirrall, 56, 57.
Holcroft, sir John, of Holcroft, 91.
Holland, John, 39.
Hollande, Rawffe, 13.
Holme, Hugh, 12.
——, Phillippe, 35.
Howarth, Theophilus, of Howarth, 84.
Humfraye, Wm., 14.
Hunter. To., 35.
Huntingdon, Henry earl of, 62.

IRELAND family, 82, 83, 88.
——, sir Gilbert, of Hutte and Hale, 52, 82; account of, 83–8.
——, Jo., of Halwood, 52.
——, Margaret, 52, 82, 83.
——, sir Thomas, of Bewsey, notices of, 49–53.
——, Thomas, his son, 50, 52, 82; notice of, 51.
——, William, 57.

JEFFERYES, John, of Acton, 49, 51, 52.
——, judge, 51.
——, Mrs., 52.
Jenison, John, 88, 93.
——, Michael, 89, 93.
Johnson, Henry, 74.
——, John, 75.
——, rev. Richard, 76, 78, 79.
——, Thomas, 75.
Jordan, Mrs., actress, 17.
Joyner, Dr., 67.

KELEY, Thomas, 74.
Killermore, co. Lanc., 12.

Kitson, sir Thomas, 62.
Kyrke, rev. Ralph, charges against, 76, 77.

LANCASHIRE, Thomas, 75.
Langton, Roger, 35.
Langtrye, Edward, notice of, 32.
——, Mrs., 34.
Lascelles, John, 60.
Lathom, Henry, 35.
Lench, Robert, 78.
Leadebeatter, Petter, 35.
——, Robert, 35.
Learoyde, rev. Mr., 77, 78.
Leghs of Lyme, 81.
Legh, sir Peter, of Lyme, 51, 58, 81, 91.
——, Piers, 90.
——, Richard, of Lyme, extracts from his letters, 84, 85, 86, 87.
Leigh, lady Dorothy, of Worsley, notices of, 80-1,
——, George, 46.
——, sir Petter, 13.
——, rev. William, funeral sermons by, 38, 39.
——, Mr., of Stoneleigh, 65.
Leicester, sir Ralph, of Toft, 48.
Leicester's Commonwealth, 20.
Lever, John, 55.
Lightboune, James, 75.
Lightoulers, James, 57.
Liverpool, vessels at, 21.
Lloyde, William, of Halton, 49.
Lloyd, Edward J., 76.
Lomax, Richard, 74, 75.
Lowe, Alexander, 54.
——, Raufe, 55.
Lownde, Raphe, 78.
Loyd, Edward, 76.
Lucas, W., 21.
Lyon, Jhon, 35.

MALOWRSARSENECK, co. Flint, 12.
Mainwaringe, William, of Ightfield, 81.
Mancringe, Mr., 31.
Man, isle of, military provision at, 21.
Manchester collegiate church, 19, 23, 76, 79.
Maney, Walter, 88, 95.
Marler, John, 74.
Marsh, George, martyr, 7.
Marston's *Masque*, 71.
Mary queen of Scots, trial and execution of, 21-3.

Mason, Gabryell, 35.
Massey, William, 13, 48.
Meutas, Hercules, 54.
Meynell, Anthony, 46.
Midle *alias* Mowld, co. Salop, 12.
Milton's *Arcades*, 72.
Molyneux family, 60-1.
——, Caryll viscount, 46.
——, Richard viscount, 60.
——, sir Richard, 91.
——, William, of Sefton, 41.
Montague, Henry earl of, 62.
Moore family, 56-8.
——, Edward, of Banck hall, notices of, 56-8.
Moore *Rental*, 58.
Morecrofte, Henry, 13.
Morgill, Edward, 59.
Morison, sir Charles, 54.
Morley, ——, 13.
——, Edward lord, 45.
Moscroppe, George, 13.
Mosley family, 54-6.
——, Francis, 74.
——, Nicholas, 74.
——, Oswald, 54, 75.
Mourning cloth, cost of, 32-5.
Murray, warden, 79.
Myldmay, sir Thomas, 3.

NAVY, book of the, 20.
Nesklyffe, co. Salop, 12.
Nestrandge, co. Salop, 12.
Newton, Marmaduke, 13.
Norfolk, Thomas duke of, 1.
Norres (of Davyhulme) family, 43.
—— (of Speke) family, 41-5; Ormerod's *Memoir*, 43-5.
——, Edward, of Speke, 41.
——, sir William, of Spcke, 57, 91.
Norris, Henry, 46.
Nugent, Walter, 74.

OGLE, Henry, of Whiston, 59.
Ogles, Mary, 52.
Orme, Richard, 39.
Ormeschurtche, Derby chapel in, 12.
Orrell, Wm., 14.
Osbaldeston, Mr., 26.
Osmownderley, co. Lanc., 12.
Otway, sir John, 75.
Otwise, Margaret, 78.
Owen, John, 80.
Oxcliffe, co. Lanc., 12.

PARKER, Edward, 13.
— Patten, William, 75.
Peckham, Edward or Edmond, 88, 93.
Pendleton, Dr., 8.
—, George, 75.
Phillips, Shakspear, 76.
Pole, John, of Radbourne, 92.
Pope, burning the, 84.
Port, sir John, 88, 91.
Pottes, Mr., 18.
Pritchard, Roger, 59.
Pycroft, Edward, 78.

RADCLIFFE, sir Alexander, of Ordsall, 48, 60.
—, Egremont, 3.
—, sir Henry, 3.
—, H., 21,
—, sir John, 4, 19, 36, 37.
—, John, lord Fitzwalter, 7.
—, Margaret, notices of, 35–7.
—, Robert, earl of Sussex, family notices of, 53–4.
—, Richard, 74.
Radley, William, 74.
Raineforth, co. Lanc., 12.
Ramsey, sir John, 54.
Reddish, Oates, 46.
Repton grammar school, 92.
Ribble water, barques in, 20.
Richardson, John, 20.
Rigby, Alexander, of Burgh, 56, 58.
Rigbye, Alexander, 13.
Robinson, Thomas, 78.
Roby's *Traditions of Lancashire*, 95.
Rushton, Ann widow of Ralph, notice of, 33.
—, Anne, 33.
—, Gefferey, 33.
Russell, Anne, 36, 37.

SALFORD assessment, (1586), 21.
Salstonstall, Richard, 55.
Samlesbury church, 6.
Scarisbrick, Edward, notice of, 32.
—, H., 21.
—, Mawd, 12.
Seager, William, Somerset herald, 28.
Seffeton, To., 35.
Selby, sir George, 61.
Seymour, William, marquis of Hertford, 61.
Sheale, Richard, extract from his *Epitaph* on lady Derby, 10.

Sherborne, John, 14.
—, sir Richard, 13, 19, 21.
Shuttleworth, Richard, of Gawthorp, 61.
Simpkin, Gerard, 75.
Skillicorne, William, 20.
Smalwood, Robert, 41.
Smyth, Symon, 35.
Somire, Edwarde, 35.
Sonkey, Edward, of Sonkey, 51.
Spencer, sir John, 62; sir John his son, 66.
Spenser, Edmund, quotation from, 68.
Stafforth, —, 13.
Stanhop, sir Michael, 54.
Stanley, Alice, 52.
—, Anne, 31, 32.
—, Dorothe, 31, 32.
—, Edward, 31, 35; his wife, 32.
—, Edward, of Moor hall, 35; notice of, 33; his wife, 34.
—, sir Edward, 13; notice of, 40, 41.
—, Francis, 13.
—, Henry, 13.
—, Henry, of Bickerstaffe, notices of, 29–35; his wife, 31.
—, James, 31.
—, Peter, of Aughton, 30.
—, Tho., 52, 61.
—, Thomas, bishop of Man, 9.
—, sir Thomas, of Auderley, 49.
—, William, 13, 14, 34.
—, sir William, of Hooton, 61.
—, Mrs., 52.
Stopforth, Claras, 14.
—, Wm., 13.
Storton, lord, 13.
—, John, 14.
—, Katherine, 13.
Sutton, Alice, 34.
—, Edward, 33.
—, William, notice of, 33.
—, Mrs., 34.

TACEY, rev. Mr., 78.
Talbot, sir John, of Salebury, 45.
—, Robert, 13.
Tarbock, Edward, of Tarbock, 42.
Thompson, John, 79.
Thorneley, co. Lanc., 12.
Thraylles, co. Lanc., 12.
Tippinge, Samuel, 74.
Torrisholme, co. Lanc., 12.
Touchet, James, 75.
—, John, 75.
Trafford, sir Edmund, notices of, 47–8.

Trevor, sir Thomas, of Trevallin, 51.
Turton, Nicholas, of Eccleshall, 57.
Tylsley, Christopher, of Morley, 42.

ULNESWALTON, co. Lanc., 12, 13.

VAVASOUR, Thomas, 14, 46.

WADINGTON, William, 35.
    Wall, William, mayor of Chester, 20.
Walle, Laurence, mayor of Preston, 20.
Wallworth, Roger, 35.
Walsingham, lady, 36.
Ward, rev. William, 52, 53.
Waring, To., 35.
Warren, Edward, 26.
Webster, Richard, 55.

Westbie, Tho., 42.
Westby, Mr., 8.
Weston, Dr., 8.
Wetton, co. Lanc., 12.
Whitaker's *Whalley*, 53.
Wilkinson, Rye., 35.
Winter, Gilbert, 76.
Witch trial, 95.
Wolsey, cardinal, 5.
Woods, George, 52.
Woodward, William, of Shevington, 39.
Worsley, Rawfe, 31.
———, Ralph, 74.
Wrightington, John, 39.
Wyer river, vessels in, 20.
Wyudlishaw, co. Lanc., 90, 91.
Wyngfeld, Mrs., 36.

YATES, Mr., 66, 75.

The Twenty-fifth Report

OF THE

COUNCIL OF THE CHETHAM SOCIETY,

Read at the Annual Meeting, held, by permission of the Feoffees, in the Audit Room of Chetham's Hospital, on the 25th of March, by adjournment from the 1st, 1868.

THE first of the publications for the year 1867-8, and the seventy-second in the Chetham Series, is *Collectanea relating to Manchester and its Neighbourhood at various periods.* Collected, arranged, and edited by JOHN HARLAND, Esq., F.S.A. Vol. II.

As this volume is of the same character as the preceding one, and has now been in the hands of the members since nearly the commencement of the current year, it is the less necessary to give an analysis or description of its contents. It brings together various interesting articles on the clubs, institutions, publications, newspapers, persons and places of Manchester, principally during the last century, which were only to be found in a scattered form in the prints of former years, and which there was a general desire to see republished in a collected shape. The result has been a most attractive miscellaneous volume, and one that affords so many curious particulars of Manchester, in its various aspects, during the period to which it refers, that to the social historian it will hereafter be a text book. Perhaps no publication of the Chetham Society, which relates to this locality, has attracted more the attention of the members, or appears to have given greater satisfaction; and should Mr. HARLAND's materials and leisure enable him to produce a supplementary volume, there can be no doubt that its appearance will be hailed as a welcome boon to the Society.

The second book for the year 1867-8, and the seventy-third in the Chetham Series, is *The Admission Register of the Manchester School, with some Notices of the more distinguished Scholars.* Edited by the Rev. JEREMIAH FINCH SMITH, M.A., Rector of Aldridge, Staffordshire, and Rural Dean. Vol. II. From A.D. 1776, to April, A.D. 1807.

The present volume brings up the list of admissions on the *Register* to the death of Lawson, and is characterized by the same persevering research and richness of biographical illustration which were so conspicuous in the preceding one. The terms used in the Report of last year with reference to that volume are therefore equally applicable to its successor; and no scholar of this time-honoured foundation who has any pride in its history or in the distinguished men it has produced, or any regard for old associations, or for that kindred feeling which knits together the generations who have been fostered under one noble scheme of comprehensive beneficence, can fail to be grateful to Mr. SMITH for his timely and most valuable labours. Had the work been postponed for a few years, the probability is that much of the information which has been procured would have been no longer attainable, and that the difficulty of collecting materials would have ultimately left the alumni of the school without an historian. This misfortune, for such it would unquestionably have been, is now averted, and the readers are safely landed, under the auspices of the editor, on the times of living memory. It is sincerely to be hoped that, great as is the sacrifice of time and attention which such a work necessarily entails, and the amount of which those only know who have been engaged in similar undertakings, he will be enabled to give us the further fruits of his researches, and to continue the notices of scholars from the death of Lawson during the period of the head-mastership of his much respected father, Dr. Jeremiah Smith.

The third and last publication for the year 1867-8, and the seventy-fourth in the Chetham Series is *Three Lancashire Documents of the Fourteenth and Fifteenth Centuries*, edited by JOHN HARLAND, Esq., F.S.A. namely:

  I. *The Great De Lacy Inquisition*, 1311.
  II. *Rental of various Manors and Places in the Hundreds of West Derby, Amounderness and Lonsdale*, 1320-46.
  III. *Custom Roll and Rental of the Manor of Assheton-under-Lyne*, 1421.

The three Documents embraced in this volume have each great value and interest, and it was suggested by the able Editor, Mr. HARLAND, that they would form a fitting volume for the Chetham Series, and at the request of the Council, and notwithstanding the pressure of the very laborious undertaking in which he was engaged, he obligingly consented to edit it for the Society. The first, which has not been printed before, is styled by Dr. Whitaker, "That most exact record, the inquisition after the death of Henry de Lacy, the last Earl of Lincoln, taken A.D. 1311," and "One of the most valuable documents from which the History of Whalley has been compiled." The second, which likewise appears for the first time, and is printed in the original Latin with a translation on the opposite page, is the remaining portion of the great Survey of 1320-46, relating to the Hundreds of West Derby, Amounderness and Lonsdale, the portion relating to the Barony and Manor of Manchester having been printed in *Mamecestre*, vol. 2. The MS. from which this important Survey is taken, was intrusted to the Rev. Canon RAINES, with permission for the Council to make any use of it they might think proper. The third, the *Custom Roll and Rental of the Manor of Ashton-under-Lyne*, 1422, was privately printed by the late Dr. HIBBERT WARE, F.R.S., as an appendix to a very interesting dissertation read by him before the Society of Scottish Antiquaries in Edinburgh, and entitled "Illustration of the Customs of a Manor in the North of England during the fifteenth Century." This appendix has become exceedingly rare, and the document itself is well worthy of being placed within the general reach of the antiquarian public. It has therefore been joined to the other two and the whole, edited by Mr. HARLAND with his usual care, will, it is conceived, be accepted as a valuable addition to the Chetham Series.

The last two volumes are nearly ready, and will be issued in the course of a few weeks to the Members.

The Council have to express their regret in recording the death of EDWARD HAWKINS, Esq., F.R.S., F.S.A., F.L.S., so long connected as a most efficient officer with the British Museum, and so well known as an accomplished numismatist and general antiquary. Mr. HAWKINS had been on the Council of the Chetham Society since its commencement, and was editor of the first work issued by the Society, *Brereton's Travels*, and of the fifteenth volume in the series, *The Lyfe and History of Saynt Werbergh*. He took considerable interest, particularly in its earlier days, in the progress and success of the Society, and was always ready to assist when applied to in obtaining materials, or in making the treasures of the British Museum accessible to the editors of its various works. Nor can the Council pass over without notice and a sincere expression of sorrow the death of Dr. RUSHTON, Vicar of Blackburn and formerly Archdeacon of Manchester, who was for some time on the Council of the Chetham Society, and only resigned that office when called to leave the neighbourhood of Manchester, and whose thorough knowledge of Lancashire localities and extensive information were always at the service of the other members of the Council.

The publications contemplated, or in progress, are:

1. *Collectanea Anglo-Poetica*, Part 4. By the Rev. THOMAS CORSER, M.A., F.S.A.

2. *The Visitation of Lancashire in 1532.* Edited by WILLIAM LANGTON, Esq.

3. *The Register of the Manchester Free Grammar School, with Notices and Biographies of distinguished Scholars.* Edited by the Rev. J. FINCH SMITH, M.A., Rector of Aldridge. Vol. 3.

4. *A Collection of Ancient Ballads and Poems, relating to Lancashire.* Edited by JOHN HARLAND, Esq., F.S.A.

5. *Worthington's Diary and Correspondence.* The concluding part. Edited by JAMES CROSSLEY, Esq., F.S.A., President of the Chetham Society.

6. *Documents relating to Edward third Earl of Derby and the Pilgrimage of Grace.* By R. C. CHRISTIE, Esq., M.A.

7. *A Selection from the Letters of Dr. Dee, with an introduction of Collectanea relating to his Life and Works.* By THOMAS JONES, B.A., F.S.A., Librarian of Chetham's Library.

8. *Tracts printed in the Controversy between Sir Thomas Mainwaring and Sir Peter Leycester, as to the legitimacy of Amicia, daughter of Hugh Cyveliok, Earl of Chester,* 1673-9. Collected and republished, with an Introductory Preface and Review of the Controversy.

9. *Diary of John Angier, of Denton, from the original Manuscripts, with a reprint of the Narrative of his Life published in* 1683 *by Oliver Heywood.*

10. *A Selection from Dr. John Byrom's unprinted Remains in Prose and Verse.*

11. *A new Edition of the Poems Collected and Published after his Death, corrected and revised, with Notes, and a Prefatory Sketch of his Life.*

12. *The later Heraldic Visitations of Lancashire.*

13. *Hollinworth's Mancuniensis.* A new Edition. Edited by CANON RAINES.

14. *A Volume of Extracts, Depositions, Letters, &c., from the Consistory Court of Chester, beginning with the Foundation of the See.*

15. *Extracts from Roger Dodsworth's Collections in the Bodleian Library at Oxford relating to Lancashire.*

16. *Annales Cestrienses.*

17. *Chetham Miscellanies.* Vol. 4.

18. *Lancashire and Cheshire Funeral Certificates.*

19. *A General Index to volumes* XXXI. *to* LX. *of the Publications of the Chetham Society.*

The Treasurer in Account with the Chetham Society, for the year ending 29th February, 1868.

DR.		L. S. D.		CR.	L. S. D.
1 Subscription for 1863-64 (21st year), reported in arrear at last meeting.			1867. Mar. 19.	Advertising	0 8 3
4 Subscriptions for 1864-65 (22nd year), reported in arrear at last meeting.				Postages	1 2 3
1 Collected		1 0 0	Aug. 27.	Fire Insurance	4 5 10
3 Outstanding.			1868. Feb. 29.	Postages	2 11 3
12 Subscriptions for 1865-66 (23rd year), reported in arrear at last meeting:				Volumes bought to make up sets	10 8 0
5 Collected		5 0 0		Advertising	0 8 3
7 Outstanding.					
17 Subscriptions for 1866-67 (24th year), reported in arrear at last meeting.					
7 Collected		7 0 0			
10 Outstanding.					
14 Subscriptions for 1867-68 (25th year), accounted for at the last meeting.					
238 Collected since		238 0 0			
50 Life Members reported at the last meeting.					
2 since dead.					
48—					
1 Commuted into Life Membership		10 0 0			
301					
49 Arrears.					
350					
12 Subscriptions for 1868-69, paid in advance		12 0 0			
Books sold to Members		32 14 6			
Book Postage received		0 1 6			
Dividends on Consols		7 6 11			
Interest from the Bank		5 18 5			
		£319 1 2			£19 3 10
Balance from last year 1st March, 1867		234 4 11		Balance to next year	534 2 3
		£553 6 1			£553 6 1

March 18th, 1869.
    Audited and found correct,
                GEORGE PEEL,
                GEORGE THORLEY, } AUDITORS.
                B. D. NAYLOR,

                                                A. H. HEYWOOD, *Treasurer.*

Chetham Society.

LIST OF MEMBERS

For the Year 1868—1869.

The Members, to whose names an asterisk is prefixed, have compounded for their Subscriptions.

*ACKERS, James, Prinknash Park, near Gloucester
  Adams, George Edward, M.A., F.S.A., Rougedragon, College of Arms, London
Agnew, Thomas, Manchester
Ainsworth, Ralph F., M.D., Manchester
Allen, Joseph, Tombland, Norwich
Andrews, Thomas, Bolton
Armitage, Samuel, Pendleton, Manchester
Armstrong, Rev. Thomas Alfred, M.A., Ashton Parsonage, Preston
Ashton, John, Warrington
Ashworth, Henry, The Oaks, near Bolton
Aspland, Alfred, Dukinfield
Aspland, Rev. R. B., Well Street, Hackney, London
Athenæum Club, London
Athenæum, Liverpool
Athenæum, Library, Boston, U.S.
*Atherton, Miss, Kersall Cell, near Manchester
Atherton, James, Swinton House, near Manchester
Atkin, William, Little Hulton, near Bolton
Atkinson, William, Ashton Heyes, near Chester
Avison, Thomas, F.S.A., Liverpool
Ayre, Thomas, Trafford Moss, Manchester

BAGSHAW, John, Manchester
  Bain, James, 1, Haymarket, London
Baker, Thomas, Brazennose Street, Manchester
*Bannerman, John, York Street, Manchester
*Barbour, Robert, Bolesworth Castle, near Chester
Barker, John, Broughton Lodge, Newton in Cartmel
*Barlow, Mrs., Greenhill, Oldham
Barratt, James, Lymm Hall, near Warrington
Barthes & Lowell, 14, Great Marlborough Street, London
Bartlemore, Miss, Beechwood, Rochdale
Barton, Richard, Caldy Manor, Birkenhead
Barton, Samuel, Whalley Range, Manchester
Beamont, William, Orford Hall, Warrington
Beever, James F., Manchester
Bentley, Rev. T. R., M.A., St. Matthew's Rectory, Manchester
Berlin Royal Library
Beswicke, Mrs., Pyke House, Littleborough
Birchall, Rev. Jos., M.A., Church Kirk, Accrington

Birmingham, Borough of, Central Free Library, Birmingham
Birley, Hugh, M.P., Moorlands, near Manchester
Birley, Rev. J. S., M.A., Halliwell Hall, Bolton
*Birley, Thomas H., Hart Hill, Eccles. Manchester
Blackburn Free Public Library and Museum
Blackburne, John Ireland, Hale, near Warrington
Bolton Public Library, Bolton-le-Moors
Booker, Rev. John, M.A., F.S.A., Sutton, Surrey
Booth, Benjamin W., Swinton, near Manchester
Booth, John, Greenbank, Monton, Eccles
Booth, William, Holly Bank, Cornbrook, Manchester
Boston, U. S., Public Library
Bourne, Cornelius, Stalmine Hall, Fleetwood, near Preston
Bower, Miss, Old Park, Bostol, Abbey wood, London S.E
Bowers, The Very Rev. G. H., D D., Dean of Manchester
Brackenbury, Miss, Brunswick Terrace, Brighton
Bradshaw, John, Jun., Manchester
*Bridgeman, Hon. and Rev. George Thomas Orlando, M A., Rectory, Wigan.
Bridson, J. Ridgway, Crompton Fold, Bolton, and Belle Isle, Windermere
Brierley, Rev. James, M A., Mosley Moss Hall, Congleton
*Brooke, Thomas, Armitage bridge, near Huddersfield
*Brooks, W. Cunliffe, M.A., F.S.A., Barlow Hall, Manchester
Brown, Mrs., Winckley Street, Preston
Browne, William Henry, Chester
Buckley, Sir Edmund, Bart., M.P., Dinas Mowddwy
Buckley, Nathaniel, F.L.S., Rochdale
Bunting, Thomas Percival, Manchester
Bury Co-operative Society, Bury, Lancashire

CAINE, Rev. William, M.A., Chaplain County Gaol, Manchester
Cambridge, Christ's College Library
Cassels, Rev. Andrew, M.A., Batley Vicarage, near Dewsbury
*Chadwick, Elias, M.A., Pudlestone Court, Herefordshire
Chichester, The Bishop of
Christie, R. C., M.A., Manchester

LIST OF MEMBERS.

*Churchill, William, Brinnington Lodge, near Stockport
*Clare, John Leigh, Liverpool
Clarke, Archibald William, Scotscroft, Didsbury
Clegg, Thomas, Manchester
Cooke, Thomas, Rusholme Hall, near Manchester
Corser, Rev. Thomas, M.A., F.S.A., Stand, near Manchester
*Cottam, Samuel, Wightwick House, Manchester
Coulthart, John Ross, Ashton-under-Lyne
*Crawford and Balcarres, The Earl of, Haigh Hall, near Wigan
Cross, William Assheton, Red Scar, Preston
Crosse, Thomas Bright, Shaw Hill, near Chorley
Crossley, George F., Beech Tree Bank, Prestwich
Crossley, James, F.S.A., Manchester, *President*
Crossley, Croslegh Dampier, Scaitcliffe House, Todmorden
Cunningham, William Alexander, Manchester

DARBISHIRE, Samuel D., Pendyffryn, near Conway
Darwell, Thomas, Manchester
Dean, Rev. Thomas, M.A., Warton, near Lancaster
Dearden, Thomas Ferrand, Rochdale
*Derby, The Earl of, Knowsley, Prescot
Delamere, The Lord, Vale Royal, near Northwich
Devonshire, The Duke of, Holker, Cartmel
Dilke, Sir C. W., Bart, 76, Sloane Street, London
Dixon, Jas., Ormskirk
Dobson, William, Preston
Downes, W. F., Manchester
Doxey, Rev. J. S, Milnrow, Rochdale
Durnford, The Ven. Richard, M.A., Rectory, Middleton, Archdeacon and Hon. Canon of Manchester

EARLE, Frederic William, Edenhurst, near Huyton
Eccles, Richard, Wigan
Eckersley, Thomas, Wigan
Egerton, Sir Philip de Malpas Grey, Bart., M.P., Oulton Park, Tarporley
Egerton, The Lord, Tatton Park, Knutsford
Ellesmere, The Earl of, Worsley Hall
Ellison, Cuthbert E., Worship Street, London
Ethelston, Rev. Hart, M.A., Cheetham Hill, Manchester

FEILDEN, Joseph, M.P., Witton, near Blackburn
*Fenton, James, M.A., F.S.A., Norton Hall, Mickleton Chipping Campden, Gloucestershire
Fernley, John, Southport
Ffarington, Miss, Worden Hall, near Preston
*Fielden, Samuel, Centre Vale, Todmorden
Fisher, William, Lancaster Banking Co., Preston
Fishwick, Major, Carr Hill, Rochdale
Fleming, William, M.D., Rowton Grange, Chester
*Fort, Richard, M.P., Read Hall, Padiham
Forster, John, Palace Gate House, Kensington, London
Frere, W. E., 42, Clarges Street, London

GARNETT, Wm. James, Quernmore Park, Lancaster
Gibb, William, Swinton Lodge, Manchester
Gladstone, Murray, F.R.A.S., Broughton, Manchester
*Gladstone, Robert, Highfield, near Manchester

Goss, Right Rev. A., D.D., St. Edward's College, Liverpool
*Greenall, Gilbert, M.P., Walton Hall, near Warrington
Greenhalgh, Rev. Henry Canon, Weldbank, Chorley

HADFIELD, George, M.P., Manchester
Hailstone, Edward, F.S.A., Horton Hall, Bradford, Yorkshire
Hardman, Henry, Bury, Lancashire
Hardy, William, F.S A., Duchy of Lancaster Office, London
Hargreaves, George J., Piccadilly, Manchester
Harland, John, F.S.A., Cheetham Hill, near Manchester
Harris, George, F.S.A., Registrar of the Court of Bankruptcy, Manchester
Harrison, William, Rock Mount, St. John's, Isle Man.
*Harrison, William, F.S.A., F G.S., F.R.S., Antq. Nord, Samlesbury Hall, near Blackburn
Harter, James Collier, Leamington
*Harter, William, Hope Hall, near Manchester
Hatton, James, Richmond House, near Manchester
Healey, Henry, Smallbridge, Rochdale
Heelis, Stephen, Manchester
*Henderson, Rev. John, Parsonage, Colne
*Henry, W. C., M.D., F.R.S., Haifield, near Ledbury
Heron, Rev. George, M.A., Carrington, Cheshire
Heywood, Arthur Henry, Manchester, *Treasurer*
Heywood, Sir Thos. Percival, Bart., Doveley's, Ashbourne
Heywood, James, F.R.S., F.G.S., 26, Palace Garden Kensington, London
Heywood, Thomas, Pendleton, near Manchester
Heywood, Rev. Henry R., M.A, Swinton, Manchester
Hickson, Charles, Manchester
Higson, James. Ardwick Green North, Manchester
Higson, John, Birch Cottage, Lees, near Oldham
Hilton, William Hughes, Booth Street, Manchester
Hoare, P. R., Kelsey Park, Beckenham, Kent
Holden, Thomas, Springfield, Bolton-le-Moors
Holdsworth, John, Eccles
*Hoghton, Sir Henry de, Bart.
Hornby, Rev. George, B.D.
Hornby, Rev. William, M.A, St. Michael's, Garstang, Hon. Canon of Manchester
Howard, Edward C., Brinnington Hall, Stockport
Howard, The Honorable Richard Edward, D C.L, Manchester
Howarth, Henry H., Castleton Hall, Rochdale
Hughes, Thomas, F.S.A., Grove Terrace, Chester
Hull, William Winstanley, The Knowle, Belper
*Hulton, Rev. C. G., M.A., Emberton, Newport Pagne Bucks
Hulton, W. A., Hurst Grange, Preston
Hume, Rev. A., LL.D., D C.L., F.S.A., Liverpool
Hutchinson, Robt. Hopwood, Tenter House, Rochdale

INDEPENDENT College, Manchester

LIST OF MEMBERS.

JACSON, Charles R., Barton Lodge, Preston
Jervis, Thomas B., Ambleside
Johnson, Jabez, Pennington Hall, near Manchester
Johnson, W. R., The Cliffe, Wybunbury, Nantwich
Jones, Jos., Abberley Hall, Stourport
Jones, Wm. Roscoe, Athenæum, Liverpool
Jones, Thomas, B.A., F.S.A., Chetham Library, Manchester
Jordan, Joseph, F.R.C.S., Manchester

KAY, Samuel, Oakley House, Weaste, Manchester
Kemp, George Awke, Rochdale
Kennedy, Jno. Lawson., Atdwick Hall, Manchester
Kershaw, James, Manchester
Kershaw, John, Cross Gate, Audenshaw, near Manchester

LANGTON, William, Manchester
Law, Wm. Bent House, Littleborough, Rochdale
Lees, Rev. William F., M.A., Sedlow Parsonage, Reigate
Legh, G. Cornwall, M.P., F.G.S., High Legh, Knutsford
*Leigh, Major Egerton, Jodrell Hall, Holmes Chapel
Leigh, Henry, Patricroft
Leigh, Miss, The Limes, Hale, near Warrington
Lingard, John R., Stockport
Lingard, Rev. R. R., M.A., Tay Bank, Dundee
Litler, H. W., Oldham
Lowndes, Edward C., Preston
*Loyd, Edward, Lillesden. Hawkhurst, Kent
*Loyd, Lewis, Monks Orchard, Bromley, Kent
Lycett, W. E., Manchester
Lyon, George, Manchester

McCLURE, William, Piccadilly, Manchester
MacKenzie, John Whiteford, Edinburgh
Makinson, A. W., 18, Abingdon Street, Westminster
Manchester Chetham Library
Manchester Free Library
*Manchester, The Bishop of
Manchester Union Club
Mann, Robert, Manchester
Mare, E. R. Le, Manchester
*Marriott, John, Liverpool
Marsden, Rev. J. H., B.D., F.R.G.S., Canon of Manchester
Marsden, G. E., Manchester
*Marsh, John Fitchett, Warrington
Mason, Hugh, Groby Lodge, Ashton-under-Lyne
Massie, Rev. E., M.A., Gawsworth Rectory, near Congleton
Master, The Ven. Archdeacon. M.A., Croston
Mayer, Joseph, F.S.A., Lord-street, Liverpool
Melbourne Public Library
Mellor, Thomas, F.R.C.S., Oxford Road, Manchester
Miller, James, Manchester and Liverpool District Bank, Manchester
Monk, John. Q.C., The Temple, London
*Mosley, Sir Oswald, Bart., Rolleston Hall, Staffordshire
*Moss, Rev. John James, Otterspool, Liverpool
Moult, William, Parkside, Prescot

Murray, James, Manchester

NAYLOR, Benjamin Dennison, Altrincham
*Neild, Jonathan, Jun., Rochdale
Newall, Henry, Hare Hill, Littleborough.
Newall, W. S., Ackworth House, Pontefract
*Newbery, Henry, Docklands, Ingatestone, Essex
Nicholson, James, F.S.A., Thelwall Hall, Warrington

ORMEROD, George, D.C.L., F.R.S., F.S.A. F.G.S., Sedbury Park, Gloucestershire
Ormerod, Henry Mere, Manchester
Owen, John, Stretford Road, Hulme, Manchester
Oxford, All Souls' College
Oxford, Brasenose College

*PARKER, Robert Townley, Cuerden Hall, near Preston
Parker, Rev. Arthur Townley, M.A., Hon. Canon of Manchester, Royle, Burnley
Parkinson, Miss, Ann's Hill, Cockermouth
Parkinson, Colonel, Eppleton Hall, Fence Houses. Durham
*Patten, Rt. Honble. J. Wilson, M.P., Bank Hall, Warrington
Pedder, Richard, Preston
Peel, George, Brookfield, Cheadle
Peel, Jonathan, Knowlmere Manor, near Clitheroe
Perris, John, Lyceum, Liverpool
Philippi, Frederick Theod., Belfield Hall, near Rochdale
*Philips, Mark, The Park, Manchester
Piccope, Rev G. J., M.A., Yarrell, Wansford, Northamptonshire
Picton, J. A., F.S.A., Clayton Square, Liverpool
Pierpoint, Benjamin, Warrington
Pitcairn, Rev. J. P., M.A., Vicarage, Eccles
*Platt, John, M.P., Werneth Park, Oldham
Pooley, W. O., Manchester
Porrett, Robert, F.R.S., F.S.A., &c., 49, Bernard Street, Russell Square, London
*Prescott, J. B.
Price, Rev. Henry H., M.A., Ash Parsonage, Whitchurch, Salop

RADFORD, Richard, Manchester
Radford, Thomas, M.D., Higher Broughton, near Manchester
Raine, Rev. James, M.A., Prebend of York
Raines, Rev. F. R., M.A., F.S.A., Vicar of Milnrow and Hon. Canon of Manchester, *Vice President*
Ramsbotham, James, Crowboro' Warren, Tunbridge Wells
Redhead, R. Milne, M.A., F.L.S., F.R.G.S., Seedley, Manchester
Reiss, Mrs., Broom House, near Manchester
Renaud, Frank, M.D., Piccadilly, Manchester
Reynolds, Rev. George W., Diocesan Church Building Society, Manchester
Rhodocanakis, H. H. The Prince, C.K.G., Ph D., F.S.A.A., F.G.H.S., Higher Broughton, Manchester
Rickards, Charles H., Manchester

LIST OF MEMBERS.

Rigby, Samuel, Bruch Hall, Warrington
*Roberts, Chas. H. Crompton, Sunnyside, Upper Avenue Road, Regent's Park, London
Roberts, Alfred Wm., Larkfield, Rochdale
Robinson, Dixon, Clitheroe Castle, Clitheroe
Robson, John, M.D., Warrington
Rochdale Library
Royds, Albert Hudson, Rochdale
Royle, Alan, Hartford Hill, near Northwich
Rushton, James, Forrest House, Newchurch
Ryle, Rev. John Charles, M.A., Stradbroke Vicarage, Suffolk

SALISBURY, Enoch Gibbon, Glan Aber, Chester
Satterfield, Joshua, Alderley Edge, near Manchester
Schofield, Wm. Whitworth, Buckley Hall, Rochdale
*Scholes, Thomas Seddon, Dale Street, Leamington
Sharp, John, Lancaster
Sharp, William, 102, Piccadilly, London
Shaw, George, St. Chad's Upper Mills, Saddleworth
Shepherd's Library, Preston
Shuttleworth, Sir J. P. Kay, Bart., M.D., Gawthorpe Hall, Burnley
Simms, Charles S., Manchester
Simpson, John Hope, Bank of Liverpool
Simpson, Rev. Samuel, M.A., Thelgreaves, near Lancaster
Sion College, The Master of, London
Skaife, John, Union Street, Blackburn
Skelmersdale, The Lord, Lathom House, near Ormskirk
Smith, Rev. J. Finch, M.A., Aldridge Rectory, near Walsall
Smith, J. R., Soho Square, London
Smith, Fereday, Manchester
Smith, R. M., Timperley
Sowler, R. S., Q.C., Manchester
Sowler, John, Manchester
Spafford, George, Brown Street, Manchester
Standish, W. S. C., Duxbury Hall, Chorley
*Stanley, The Lord, Knowsley, Prescot, and The Albany, London
*Stanley of Alderley, The Lord, Alderley, Congleton
Stradbroke Vicarage, Suffolk
Sudlow, John, Manchester
Swindells, G. A. Ancoats Grove, Manchester

TABLEY, The Lord de, Tabley House, Knutsford
Tate, Wm. James, Manchester
Tatton, Thos., W. Wythenshawe Hall, Cheshire
*Taylor, James, Todmorden Hall, Todmorden
Taylor, James, Whiteley Hall, Wigan
Taylor, John, Moreton Hall, Whalley
Taylor, Mrs. T., Knutsford
Taylor, Rev. W. H., M.A., Farnworth

Taylor, Thomas Frederick, Wigan
Teale, Josh., F.R.C.S., Salford
Thicknesse, Rev. F. H., M.A., Hon. Canon of Manchester, Deane Vicarage, Bolton
*Thompson, Joseph, Woodlands, Fulshaw
Thompson, James, Chronicle Office, Leicester
Thorley, George, Manchester
Thorp, Henry, Manchester
Threlfall, Richard, Hollowforth, Preston
*Tootal, Edward, The Weaste, Eccles
Tonge, Rev. Richard, M.A., The Rectory, Heaton Mersey
Townend, John, Shadsworth Hall, Blackburn
Towneley, Colonel Chas., F.S.A., Towneley Park, Burnley
Trafford, Sir Humphrey de, Bart., Trafford Park, Manchester
Turner, Thomas, F.R.C.S, Manchester
Turner, Rt. Rev. W., D.D., Crescent, Salford
Tweedale, A. A., Spring Cottage, near Rochdale

VAUGHAN, John Lingard, Stockport
Vitré, Edward Denis de, M.D., Lancaster

WANKLYN, James H., Manchester
Wanklyn, William Trevor, Manchester
Warburton, R. E. Egerton, Arley Hall, near Northwich
Ward, Edmund, Holly House, Prescot
*Ward, Jos. Pilkington, Whalley Range, Manchester
Ware, Titus Hibbert, Hale Barns, Altrincham
Westhead, Joshua P. B., Lea Castle, Kidderminster
*Westminster, The Marquis of, Eaton Hall, Chester
Wheeler, Benjamin, Manchester
Whitaker, Rev. Robert Nowell, M.A., Vicar of Whalley
Whitaker, W. W., St. Ann's Street, Manchester
Whitehead, James, M.D., Manchester
Whitelegg, Rev.William, M.A., Hulme, Manchester
Whittaker, Rev. Robt., M.A., Leesfield, Oldham
Whitworth, Robert, Courtown House, Manchester
Wilkinson, Eason Matthew, M.D., Manchester
Wilkinson, T. T., Cheapside, Burnley
*Wilton, The Earl of, Heaton House, near Manchester
Wood, Richard Henry, F.S.A., Crumpsall, Manchester, *Honorary Secretary*
Woods, Albert W., F S.A., Lancaster Herald, College of Arms, London
Wood, Richard, Cornville House, Whalley Range, Manchester
Worthington, Edward, 23, Ladbroke Garden, London

YATES, Edward, Liverpool
York Subscription Library, York
Young, Sir Charles G., F.S.A., Garter King of Arms, London

The Honorary Secretary requests that any change of address may be communicated to him or to the Treasurer.

www.ingramcontent.com/pod-product-compliance
Lightning Source LLC
Chambersburg PA
CBHW020117170426
43199CB00009B/554